NAVIGA
POLAR

Using Both/And Thinking
to Lead Transformation

Brian Emerson & Kelly Lewis

P A R A D O X I C A L
P R E S S

Washington, DC

Paradoxical Press
Washington, D.C.

Soft copies of The Polarity Navigator are available for free download at
www.navigatingpolarities.com.

Special discounts for bulk quantities are available to corporations and
other organizations. Contact www.paradoxicalpress.com for details and
information.

Library of Congress Cataloging-in-Publication Data
Emerson, Brian, 1967-
Navigating polarities : using both/and thinking to lead transformation /
Brian Emerson and Kelly Lewis.
pages cm
Includes bibliographical references.
ISBN 978-1-7333828-3-0
1. Leadership. 2. Problem solving. I. Lewis, Kelly Cook. II. Title.
LCCN 2019912961

LC record available at https://lccn.loc.gov/2019912961

Cover design by James Ulysse
Editing, Typesetting and Marketing Support by Archangel Ink

HELPFUL RESOURCES

Blank Polarity Navigator and Navigator Tool

While working through this book many people find it helpful to have a blank Polarity Navigator as a resource. You can download free copies of the Navigator Tool at www.navigatingpolarities.com.

CONTENTS

ACKNOWLEDGMENTS

This book was many years in the making and was made possible by the many brilliant and loving people we've had the privilege to learn with and from, directly and indirectly. Our life-giving community of teachers, friends, family, colleagues, and clients shaped our thinking and practice in significant ways, and we hope they see this work as a worthy extension of their own contribution and legacy.

We must begin with Barry Johnson, who introduced the world to Polarity Theory and taught us both about the powerful energy contained in polarities. Barry, your generous spirit, passionate heart, and abiding commitment to supplementing the thinking on the planet with both/and inspires our dedication to more effectively navigate polarities in our own lives while helping others do the same. Thank you for the indelible impact you've had on our work and lives.

Anita Cook, Kelly's mom. Thank you for allowing me to accompany you as you navigated life's most precious paradox — life/death. Our time together showed me the essential role vulnerability and spirit play in embracing the contradiction and ultimately standing in the Third Way. I am eternally grateful for your courage and grace and in constant awe of what each moment offers when I can be present to what already is.

This series was the brainchild of Elaine Yarbrough. Thank you for sparking the idea and for your continuous encouragement to pursue it. Your zest for life and passion for learning are contagious.

Nancy Wallis was central to Brian's research that developed the theories of Suffering Paradox and Navigating Paradox. Thank you for your support, friendship, and ongoing nudge to bring this to the world.

We have been fortunate to share in a process of inquiry and exploration of polarities with two communities of polarity practitioners. The first is the group of our fellow Polarity Mastery graduates. We deeply appreciate the shared learning experience with our respective cohorts – Mastery 3 and Mastery 6. Thank you for bringing yourselves, your challenges, and your work to the table and making space for us to do the same. Thank you to the entire Polarity Mastery Community, especially Cliff Kayser, Elaine Yarbrough, Beena Sharma, and Margaret Seidler. We are honored to join you all in the mission of sharing this important work with others.

The second community is the growing group of graduates from the Navigating Polarities Executive Certificate Program at Georgetown University. We are sincerely grateful to the members of Cohorts 1 and 2: Anne Nagle, Betsy Miller, Carole Tilmont, Cleo Haynal, Janis Timberlake, Jim Massey, John Reifsnider, Katie Lackey, Kerstin Hess, Nancy Wallis, Randy Chittum, Sharon Blackborow, Sheryl Phillips, Sukari Pinnock, Susan Nester, Amber Roos, Amy Levine, Barbara Roswell, Debs Weinberg, Deiadre Rauch, Jan Nelson, Jiji George, Julie McKee, Kim Weinberg, Matt Dawson, Sharon Harrington, and Tonio Verzone. Thank you for choosing to learn along with us in service of your own development and the development of your clients, teams, and organizations. It has been a tremendous privilege and provided us with a platform to continue the development of this body of work.

We are humbled to be part of these two generative communities of scholars and practitioners and are lucky to have close personal relationships and collaboration with so many that share in the commitment of improving our quality of life by supplementing either/or with both/and. If some of their language may have unconsciously slipped in without attribution because of shared tradition, countless conversations, and an ongoing inquiry and exploration of Polarity and Paradox Theory, we intend this as a blanket apology and as heartfelt appreciation and acknowledgment of their work and the ways it has impacted our lives. Webs of learning partnerships, friendships, family, and chosen family have nourished and inspired us along the way. Special gratitude to Michael Milano, John Reifsnider, John Frisch, Betsy Miller, and Tonio Verzone for your generosity, thoughtfulness, and rich feedback. Loving thanks to Kate Ebner, Carole Tilmont, Amy Su, Sharon Blackborow, Anne Nagle, John Pullen, Ann Deaton, Dawn Coleman, Jimmy Chou, Whitney Forstner, Katie Lackey, and Patrick Masterson for the wholehearted conversations and support that have contributed to the fabric of our thoughts, actions, and being in the world.

The work of getting a book into the hands of readers goes well beyond the authors. We have heartfelt gratitude for Jenny Patterson, who serves as the backbone to what we do in the world. Thank you for making our work possible. Additional thanks to Tessa McCawley for shepherding the publishing process, Lisa Dorsey and Cole Pellicano for the support they provided, and Erica Ellis, our editor, whose insight was an invaluable gift to the process.

This journey, and all of its unexpected twists and turns, has served as one of our most important learning partners. We can, now, genuinely express our appreciation for the process itself. It invited us to listen to what this book wanted to become and let go of what we expected it was going to be. It challenged us to find the Third Way between Responsibility::Forgiveness, Patience::Persistence, Take It Seriously::Hold It Lightly, and Humility::Confidence and confirmed for us that when we honor both, and eliminate neither, transformation is possible.

Our deepest gratitude goes, finally, to our partners in life – Chris Lorence and Glenn Lewis. The way the two of you tirelessly love, encourage, and support us makes us better people. Your belief in us has expanded our belief in ourselves individually and as a team. You inspire us to think big and love deeply, and we are forever grateful to share the adventure of life and growth with you.

INTRODUCTION

You've experienced it. We all have. The need to choose between two "opposites" when neither, by itself, seems quite right. The need to strike a balance between two states, when doing so seems a bit impossible.

- Evan is stuck. Should he keep his structured approach or give people more freedom and empowerment?
- Maria is struggling. Should she say what's really on her mind or worry about damaging her relationships?
- Malachi is in a quandary. Does he help his daughter finish a top-notch project or let her struggle to learn on her own?
- Amanda is torn. Should she collaborate during the negotiation or draw a hard line in the sand?

These are paradoxes, dilemmas, no-wins, tough choices, the space between the hard place and the rock, and we've all been there. In our work with thousands of people across the globe, we have seen these tensions, which we call polarities, create stress at the intrapersonal level, in relationships, on teams, in organizations, and in society. *And*, we have seen many of those same people harness and use these tensions to achieve incredible results and create positive energy.

When they know how.

Our goal in writing this book, and in editing this series, is to explore a tool and way of making sense of the world that we've used with countless people and organizations to effectively navigate polarities. We've seen it reduce the suffering and wasted energy often resulting from the types of issues mentioned above so that people can spend more time focusing on success—better results, bigger impact, improved morale, deeper relationships. In short, a better world. We've seen these concepts drive richer conversations and action in both our lives and the lives of our clients which, for us, is both exciting and life-giving.

Dealing with paradox in organizations and leadership has received significant focus in both the popular and academic literature during the past several decades. The growing complexity of organizations, and the interconnectedness of the global marketplace, has magnified the frequency with which organizations and leaders are expected to navigate seemingly unsolvable situations containing two or more opposing solutions. For example:

- Driving to meet individual team goals while collaborating with other teams to do what's best for the whole.
- Making time for developing employees while working faster to achieve more output.
- Focusing on what's best for the bottom line while doing what's best for the environment.
- Providing clear direction and structured processes while encouraging flexibility and innovation.

There is no shortage of literature that laments the difficulty of dealing with these paradoxical situations, also known as polarities, dualities, dialectics, wicked problems, etc., or that discusses the growing importance for leaders and organizations to deal with them effectively. Likewise, research and history have shown that organizations, leaders, and even societies that harness the "power of the and" do better, over time, than those that operate solely with an "either/or mentality".[1] In fact, some say that knowing how to handle paradox and operate with a "both/and mentality" is among the top skills needed by leaders in our modern time.[2]

Unfortunately, while there has been a lot of talk *about* paradox, there are few who provide practical solutions about *what to do* with paradox or *how* to successfully manage it. Therein lies the need for, and purpose of, this book and the series that follows.

This series demonstrates, in practical terms, how to navigate *polarities – paradoxical situations in which two seemingly opposite yet interdependent states need to coexist over time in order for success to occur.* These interdependent pairs are everywhere and are never going away. Although we can't solve them, or power our way through them (though many of us try!), we *can* learn to navigate them in a way that harnesses the creative tension inherent in them all. This book outlines a practical way to do just that.

Polarities are not new. They are older than humankind and have been a driving force in cultures throughout history. Until recently, however, making sense of these polarities was often left to chance. There was no practical or explicit way to examine the two poles and take action to harmonize them or find the Third Way between them. It was as if we were victim to the polarities. They "had" us; we didn't "have" them. It was difficult to make sense of them, let alone know how to navigate them to harness their creative tension.

That began to change when Barry Johnson developed the concept of The Polarity Map®, a sensemaking tool that outlines a way in which we can intentionally navigate and use polarities for good. [3] His idea of creating a map has helped countless individuals, teams, organizations, and communities make sense of polarities in a way that leads to faster change and more sustainable results—all while generating a positive energy that drives deeper connections and trust.

Our two decades working with Barry, coupled with our own research and learning from other practitioners and scholars, as well as our lived experience in our coaching and client work, led to the development of the Polarity Navigator. The Navigator is a sensemaking tool that stands squarely on the shoulders of Barry's work while allowing for the exploration of the reintegration of the poles and the vulnerability it takes to stand in the tension of paradox, two topics we feel are vital to the conversation about polarities. This series builds on these concepts and introduces other new approaches used in the field by polarity and paradox practitioners.

We chose to write a series to deal with several polarities faced by all authors and teachers:

- Do you cover a topic with breadth, or do you aim for depth and dig into the specifics?
- Do you focus on the practical or the theoretical?
- Do you shoot for something short that people can use quickly or something long that people can sink their teeth into?

It is our hope that examining the topic of polarities through a series enables us to effectively say "yes" to all of those choices. This initial book outlines what polarities are, how to make practical sense of them, and how to navigate them for sustained success. The follow-up books, written by practitioners and thought leaders in the field, cover a myriad of ways that the wisdom of polarities can be applied to real life. Each begins with the assumption that the reader knows about polarities and how to leverage them (i.e., has read this book or attended a workshop of some sort).

We begin the first book by discussing what polarities are, the impact they can have on human systems, and some of the research about the effects of managing them well. In Chapter 2, we lay out the predictable and formulaic manner in which all polarities work. This allows us to examine the role that vulnerability and courage play in stepping into the Third Way to navigate and harness the creative tension inherent in all polarities.

Chapter 3 is the practical how-to guide of using the Polarity Navigator. Chapter 4 provides the five-step process of navigating polarities and presents several high-level examples and cases of how the Polarity Navigator has been used in various organizations (many more of these follow in the books in this series).

Perhaps the most difficult skill of using polarities is the ability to see them — to understand when a situation or issue is the result of a polarity at play. This skill is highlighted in Chapter 5, for without it the rest of this book is rather useless. Finally, we'll end by looking at how polarities impact personal and systems change. Our research, work, and lived experience has shown that using polarities as a framework to make sense of, and embody, paradoxical tensions is a powerful and often transformational process. It allows us to Navigate Paradox instead of suffering through it and can show us how to turn our desperate either/ors into vibrant both/ands. It enables us to see ourselves, others, and the world around us more fully, thus making it possible to accept and embrace our many contradictions. Our hope is that this series helps drive different conversations in the world so that we, as a planet, can experience the benefits available when we Navigate Paradox.

CHAPTER 1

WHAT ARE POLARITIES AND WHY SHOULD WE CARE?

The world is filled with either/or choices. We can do either this or that. Situations are either black or white. It's easy to identify ourselves and others based on which side of the "or" we land on, such as:

- Either I eat meat or I'm a vegetarian.
- Either she's allergic to cats or she's not.
- Either we'll hire person A or we'll hire person B.
- Either I'll be candid or I'll be diplomatic.
- Either you're a big-picture person or you're a details person.
- Either I hold people accountable or I cut them some slack.

Wait. If you're like most people, by the time you got to the last three items on the list, you were probably thinking, "Hold on, can't someone be a little bit of both? You can't be just all of one without some of the other." That's the point.

The first three examples on the list are either/or choices. One choice does not depend on the other, per se, so we can be all of one (a vegetarian) without being any of the other (a meat eater). They can be approached with either/or thinking, a vital skill for addressing the problems we face in the world. Problems typically involve either/or choices with a "right" and a "wrong" solution. Once we figure it out, it's solved, and we can move on to the next thing. Deciding to hire person B might be a very tough choice involving many complex variables, but once the problem is solved and the decision is made, you can move on and get back to business as usual.

This isn't the case for the last three examples on the list, which are actually interdependent. They rely on one another and if we want to be successful in the long term, we can't be all of one without being at least a bit of the other. They are not either/or choices—they require us to think both/and.

- We need both candor and diplomacy.
- We need both big-pictures and details.
- We need both accountability and forgiveness.

These are polarities—seemingly opposite states that must coexist over time for success to occur. Their interdependence requires both/and thinking. If we ignore one in light of the other over the long term, we end up in a bad situation. For example, we couldn't live in a world if there were no candor. We couldn't survive if we never paid attention to the details. There would be chaos if there were no accountability. A key here is "over time." It might be possible to focus on just one pole in the short term, but in the long run, if we want to be successful, we'll need both.

Problem vs. Polarity

Problem	Polarity
A question or puzzle that needs to be solved	A situation in which two interdependent and seemingly contradictory states must be maintained for success over time

Figure 1.1

In the lives of our clients, they have shown up like this:

- Should we do what's best for the bottom line or what's best for the environment?
- Should we draw a hard line in the sand or worry about being diplomatic?
- Should we honor our partner's need for collaboration or maintain our competitive spirit?
- Should we keep things open and flexible to maintain our entrepreneurial spirit or introduce structure and processes to drive consistency?
- Should we customize to meet the individual needs of local regions or standardize to do what's best for the global enterprise?

What's the right answer? Naturally, it depends on the context, but the best answer is most likely, "both." This seems obvious when looking at the written page but, in the real world, these questions often create vigorous debates at best, and at worst they cause unhealthy tension, animosity, and suffering. People quickly take sides, create camps, dig in their heels, and then start pushing against "the enemy." Even though we know, intellectually, that we need both, for some reason people get triggered and work (sometimes vigorously) to protect their point of view. This results in one group pushing *this* way while the other group pushes *that* way, and before long, everyone is stuck going nowhere. Nothing happens. Take the United States Congress as a case in point.

We are sometimes asked whether there is a difference between a polarity and a paradox. While deeper analysis of these words does reveal some differences, the two words are often used interchangeably in this field, and we are using them that way as well.

Some Common Polarities

Here is a list of *some* common polarities (there are more in Appendix A, page 157). Think about the multiple ways these play out inside organizations and society. More importantly, consider the impact these polarities have when individuals or groups emphasize one pole over the other.

Some Polarities in Organizations

Structure::Flexibility
Employee Interests::Organizational Interests
Continuity::Change
Decentralization::Centralization
Focus on Margin::Focus on Mission
Short-term Focus::Long-term Focus
Participative Leadership::Directive Leadership
Focus on Costs::Focus on Quality

Some Polarities in Leadership

Exude Confidence::Exude Humility
Action::Reflection
Challenge::Support
Focus on Task::Focus on Relationship
Candor::Diplomacy
Implementation::Planning
Grounded::Visionary
Develop Bonds::Maintain Distance

Some Polarities in Life

Work::Rest
Hold Lightly::Take Seriously
Appreciate What Is::Desire More
Focus on Self::Focus on Other
Responsibility::Forgiveness
Reality::Hope
Being Open::Being Assured
Save::Spend

Polarities: Interdependent Pairs

The interdependence of polarities stems from the philosophical argument that polarities are two sides of the same coin that spark the question, *could one exist without the other?* If there were no fast, would there be a slow? If there were no work, would there be play? If we didn't have structure would there be flexibility? The poles are interdependent because one would not exist without the other—in fact, one actually creates the other.

Take this illusion as an example. When looking at it for the first time, many people immediately see a tree while others see two faces. Fairly quickly, most people come to see both because it's an interdependent image—the faces create the tree and, yet, the tree creates the faces. It's easy to see both here, but it's just as easy to extrapolate this to real life, with real issues, where people get locked into their perspective. It's a tree. No, it's faces. No, you're wrong—IT'S A TREE!!! And the debate begins, each trying to prove their point until someone stops them and says, "Hey, actually…we've got to have both!"

The Pendulum Swing

Unfortunately, this tension plays out all too often in relationships, organizations, and society where situations that require both/and thinking are treated as either/or problems to solve. One common way to deal with them is to swing the pendulum from one pole to the other without realizing the "Hey, actually…it's both!" Here are some examples we've heard from clients:

- We were centralized when I started working here, then about three years ago, we decentralized. Now our new leader wants us to centralize again.

- We used to focus on employee development, but the budget got a little tight so now we just focus on the bottom line.

- We got things under control by implementing clear processes, but now we're so slow that nothing's getting done. We need to make things more flexible to drive innovation.

- We need more collaboration, so we're going to break down all the silos and become one big team.

These scenarios create real tension as people take sides, draw lines in the sand, and get stuck in debates that detract focus from the ultimate mission of their organization. As the pendulum swings, precious resources are wasted implementing solutions that aren't sustainable in the long term because, as most will tell you, "Just wait…the pendulum will swing back!"

A polarity mindset allows us to transcend the pendulum. It helps us think—and perhaps, more importantly, it helps us *help others think*—about how we might get the best of both options. Not a compromise to the situation, but an approach that embodies the benefits of both poles. It allows for different conversations so that we don't dig in our heels and stop listening. It helps us develop different solutions that are more sustainable and more successful in the long run. It helps us see the world more completely and, like the illusion above, once we see both sides, it's virtually impossible to unsee them.

While the concept of polarities can seem elementary, the fact is, they can damage relationships, negatively impact results, and be the cause of much suffering in the world. So how can we help ourselves, our teams, our organizations, and our societies strike the right balance? How do we dance on both sides of the spectrum when we need to? How can we ask the kinds of questions that drive dialogue, instead of polarized bickering, so the system can find the answers it needs? A polarity mindset offers a way, which we'll examine step-by-step in the coming chapters. However, before getting there, it's important to make sure we are not demonizing either/or thinking, and to understand why both/and thinking can sometimes be difficult to practice.

The Importance of Either/Or

To be clear, we are not advocating that both/and thinking is, in some way, superior to either/or thinking. Both are vital because *not everything is a polarity*. The world is filled with problems that need to be solved and either/or thinking is needed to solve them. Both/and thinking supplements either/or thinking, it doesn't replace it. This is critical.

- To survive, we need either/or thinking—when the building we're in is on fire, we can *either* stay *or* get out.
- To keep society together, we need either/or thinking—when we see something we like in a shop, we can *either* steal it *or* respect the shop owner and pay for it.
- To thrive, we need either/or thinking—when we look at our finances, we can *either* end the year with more expenses *or* more income.

To assume that either/or thinking is somehow less important than both/and thinking is shortsighted.

Either/or thinking is so essential, in fact, that we educate people to refine it and reward their innate capacity for it. In school, this answer is good, that answer is bad. That is correct, this is not acceptable. The hypothesis is valid, or it is not valid. We teach people to be really good either/or thinkers, which is brilliant, because people need to be. That's not the issue. The problem comes when people are thrown into a world where they need to supplement either/or thinking with a both/and mindset. Unfortunately, by then, our minds are so trained on the either/or that we naturally pick sides in situations that need both sides for success.

It would be easy to interpret some literature of the past decade as suggesting both/and thinking might be, in some way, more desirable than either/or thinking. However, we disagree, for either/or thinking and both/and thinking are themselves a polarity to be leveraged. Neither, without the other, is a successful approach in the long term. To thrive, we need both.

Polarities Aren't New

It's also important to acknowledge that none of this is new. Polarities and interdependent pairs have been around for as long as the world has existed. In the East, there is the concept of yin and yang, and in the West, Aristotle and Plato both contended that the universe is composed of opposites. Many of Aristotle's virtues focus on taking two opposite extremes and maintaining the right blend of both. The major religions of the world are rife with polarities such as Justice and Mercy or Works and Grace. Smith and Lewis[1] write extensively about paradoxical tensions inside of organizations and leadership. Geert Hofstede[2] has identified interdependent tensions at play in major national cultures (Masculine and Feminine, Individual and Collective, etc.). However, regardless of their abundant and eternal presence, it seems as though polarities are harder to see, understand, and navigate than we might expect.

The Difficulty with Developing Both/And Thinking

As attractive and important as it might be to embrace polarities and hold a both/and mindset, it's an endeavor easier said than done. The task is harder than we might like because, to some degree, the decks are stacked against us. Our hardwiring, our language, and the evolving way we make sense of the world all seem to conspire against our best efforts to see the world with a both/and mindset.

From an evolutionary perspective, the brain is masterful at either/or thinking, and it doesn't like the nebulousness of both/and. From the earliest times, the brain has had to quickly determine if something was safe *or* dangerous. The brain focuses the eyes on the foreground *or* on the background. When there's work to be done, we have to decide whether to do it now *or* do it later. The brain craves predictability, either to keep a few steps ahead or simply to be able to focus mental energy on something more important. Seeing things in opposition is hardwired into our brains, which makes it completely logical and understandable that we would have to work harder to hold a both/and mentality.

This is compounded by the fact that the language we use further conspires to keep us thinking in opposition.

- stability and change
- structure and flexibility
- candor and diplomacy

Obviously, the common word in these three polarities is "and." However, in our experience, it is easy — common, in fact — to replace the word "and" with "versus" or "or." People often speak of:

- stability *vs.* change
- structure *vs.* flexibility
- candor *vs.* diplomacy

This, of course, sets up the pair as a confrontation or in competition with a winner and loser. You might have even noticed a slight difference in your body as you read the two different lists. In the second set, there is a struggle, and we have to choose a side. This language reinforces an either/or mindset that's extremely difficult to overcome.

Additionally, our languages (English, especially) do not adequately reflect the world's need for a both/and mentality. We do not have language to express the combination or harmonization of the two seemingly opposite states that must coexist over time for success to occur. We lack language for the integration of specific poles, or what we call the Third Way. Consider this example:

This is a nut.

This is a bolt.

What do we call this?

Some will say it's a "fastener," which is only partially accurate because staples and buttons are also fasteners. If this object were lying on a table alongside a staple and a button and someone asked for the "fastener," which one would they want? While a nut and bolt are *not* a polarity, the lack of a name for the combination of the two demonstrates a reason why it can be difficult to see both/and.

The fact that we have no word for the nut *and* bolt together means that we can only talk about, or make sense of, them as two distinct objects that sometimes join together. This dilemma is incredibly limiting. What do we call a leader who harmonizes competition with collaboration? What do we call it when an organization balances decentralization and centralization? Structure and flexibility? Some would argue that not having words for these states means that we are incapable of seeing or understanding them fully.

This is why we use the double colon :: between the poles when writing out the name of a polarity (e.g., Compete::Collaborate) and when speaking, pronounce them without a connecting word (e.g., Structure Flexibility). Using the word "and" continues to separate the poles and hold them as two distinct entities. Replacing the word "and" with :: allows for the closest representation of concepts that are simultaneously distinct *and* connected which, for us, is more symbolic of a polarity and the Third Way.

To continue the examples above, when providing feedback to an employee, we can tell them to "be more candid." But they might ask, "How much more?" If we had a word for the magic mix of "candidly diplomatic" (the nut *and* the bolt), then we could simply tell them to be that and call it a day. Not having a word to describe the state makes it difficult to pinpoint exactly what we're talking about. And simply telling them to "balance candor and diplomacy" might also be problematic because research suggests a significant portion of adults see the world in a binary way that makes "balancing" seem somewhat impossible. [3]

According to scholars and practitioners who utilize adult development stage theory, the majority of adults make sense of the world in a way that predisposes them to binary, black/white, either/or thinking.[4] The shift from primarily either/or thinking to naturally include more both/and thinking is a significant mental expansion that doesn't happen until later stages of development. It first requires us to shift from seeing a world filled with independent variables to seeing interdependent variables and then to make another shift to making sense of the world as independent AND interdependent variables. The majority of adults do not do this unassisted. Therein lies the need for a sensemaking tool, a map, if you will, that helps people understand and Navigate Paradox and interdependent pairs.

Barry Johnson[5] created his initial Polarity Map and principles in 1975. His work allowed people to map polarities in order to understand and leverage interdependent pairs. Building on his work, the Polarity Navigator helps individuals, groups, and organizations make sense of polarities and the Third Way that comes from their integration. As Kegan would say, this allows us to make *object* polarities to which we might otherwise be *subject*.[6]

When we are subject to something, it's like a pair of glasses we don't even realize we're wearing. The glasses shape and tint how we see and act in the world without us realizing it. When we become aware of the glasses and take them off, hold them out, and examine them, we make them object. This allows *us* to have the glasses instead of *them* having us. We have made object our way of seeing. This opens the option and freedom to choose when, and if, to put the glasses on (or to select a different pair of glasses!) because we have more distance from them—we are now aware of them and have more control over them.

The Polarity Navigator can help make a polarity object. This enables us to do a better job of managing the inherent tension because *we have it, it doesn't have us.* Fair warning—we use that phrase a lot! The Navigator helps provide distance to see more fully how the dynamic is impacting our actions and the situation we're in. Through this increased understanding, we can make intentional choices to act in ways that harness the inherent tension of interdependent pairs and use it for creativity and good. But why should we care? Why can't we just leave all of this to its natural state and let things play out as they will?

Benefits of Understanding Polarities

There are numerous benefits to effectively navigating polarities. Holding a both/and mindset to deal with contradictory demands has been linked to individual career success, exceptional leadership, high-performing groups, and overall organizational success.[7] In this section, we explore another key reason to better understand how polarities work—to turn the inherent tension into a creative force and not a destructive one.

The two poles in any interdependent pair are constantly pulling in seemingly opposite directions, creating an ongoing tension. In the Structure and Flexibility polarity, for example, one pole is pulling toward maintaining order, while the other is pulling toward freedom. This tension is neither good nor bad but, depending on how the energy is managed, it can turn creative or destructive and positively or negatively impact a system, respectively. Understanding how to navigate polarities and harness this tension helps individuals, teams, and organizations reap the ancillary benefits that come as a result of managing a polarity well and avoid the negative ripples that occur when it's done poorly. By having a way to make sense of polarities, we can be intentional about how we approach the polarity so that we have it, it doesn't have us—the latter of which is, unfortunately, all too often the case.

Suffering Paradox

According to our research,[8] when groups encounter a polarity and don't have a way to make sense of it, or understand it as an interdependent pair, they go through a series of stages (Preferencing, Attaching, Othering, Either/Or-ing) called Suffering

Paradox [see Figure 1.2 on the following page]. In this case, the tension that is a natural part of the polarity turns destructive and impacts not only the issue at hand but other areas of the organization as well.

If people have no way to make sense of the polarity and approach it with an either/or mindset, they quickly enter the Preferencing stage in which they place more value on one pole over the other, even though they might know both poles are important. No matter the reason for the preference — personality, upbringing, past experiences — they start to see the issue from that perspective.

If people in a group are unable to see their preferences as interdependent, the tension can build and people begin Attaching themselves to a particular point of view — so much so that they can begin to adopt their point of view as part of their personality, claiming things like "I am a big-picture person," "I'm all about change," or "I am a process guy." Their point of view can become part of their identity or ego and how they make sense of themselves in the world.

Suffering Paradox

| Inferior Results | Decreased Morale | Hampered Communication | Damaged Relationships |

1. Preferencing
Giving preference to one pole over the other

2. Attaching
Wedding oneself to a pole (at all costs)

3. Othering
Creating "the Other" to personify the tension

4. Either/Or-ing
Problem solving from an either-or mindset

Figure 1.2

When people who are attached to a perspective bump up against others who hold the "opposite" perspective, they can get resistant and even recalcitrant as the things they value, and thereby their identity, are being threatened. This questioning of identity becomes a big determinant in how we deal with paradox. The threat to the ego can trigger responses in the brain that drive people to protect themselves and, in turn, lower their willingness to be open and vulnerable to other ways of seeing and being.

This can lead to Othering, which is when we seek to make the other point of view wrong in order to validate our perspective and who we see ourselves to be. People can begin to demonize others, blame each other for the standstill, and dig in their heels to prove they're right. They then take sides for or against the issue at hand and begin Either/Or-ing, where one side wins and the other loses. Unfortunately, not only will the solution the group chooses not be successful over time (e.g., because the pendulum will inevitably swing back and they will "decentralize" again), they are also left with the byproducts of the destructive tension created during the process.

When this happens, the system gets stuck and a vicious cycle can begin in which groups become entrenched, lose momentum, and make no progress. In addition, there are ripple effects created that extend well beyond the issue at hand and wreak havoc in ways that have nothing to do with the polarity being encountered. The political systems of many countries around the world are cases in point.

Our research suggests that when groups Suffer Paradox, they are also negatively impacted in the areas of communication, morale, results, and relationships. Communication issues and low morale seep into areas beyond those most directly related to the polarity and negatively impact results and effectiveness. Perhaps more importantly, relationships can be damaged, making the group less cohesive and prepared to tackle future issues as they arise.

But it doesn't have to be this way.

Navigating Paradox

What our research also uncovered is that when a group understands polarities, the tension in the dynamic can turn into a creative force instead of a destructive one. Having the ability to make sense of a paradoxical situation through the lens of polarities helps groups have it instead of it having them. When this happens, they can be intentional about how they approach and deal with the situation and its interdependent pair in order to reap other rewards as well.

Groups that use a sensemaking tool to see the situation with a polarity mindset know that the issue is not solvable. They understand that an issue consisting of interdependent pairs can only be navigated over time, that they will not be able to settle on one right solution that can be implemented and then forgotten about. They understand that the tension is ongoing and that they can intentionally manage it so that it turns creative, or it will manage them by turning destructive.

When a group encounters an issue that involves interdependent pairs and they use a tool to make sense of the polarity, they experience the stages that have come to be known as Navigating Paradox. These stages are known as Mapping, Divining, Synergizing, and Both/And-ing [see Figure 1.3 below]. By Mapping the polarity, they are able to consciously make object an interdependent pair to which they might otherwise have unwittingly been subject.

Through Mapping, they enter the stage known as Divining, in which several interesting things happen. First, like a divining rod that shows the way, a map of a polarity allows a group to predict what will happen if they approach the issue from only one perspective, and it helps explain the past by showing how the over-focus on one pole has led to the current situation. Secondly, groups that map polarities often suggest there is something almost magical that can happen inside a group that would otherwise be experiencing negative tension—thus, the term *Divining*. People begin to listen to each other, conversations become richer, and they have more courage to step into the vulnerability needed to look at their identity. As a result, a dialogue starts that allows people to see the situation, and each other, more completely.

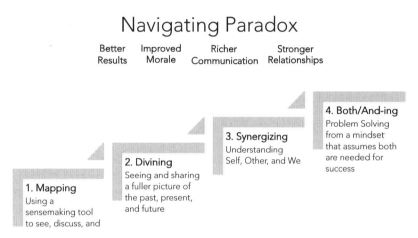

Navigating Paradox

| Better Results | Improved Morale | Richer Communication | Stronger Relationships |

1. Mapping
Using a sensemaking tool to see, discuss, and

2. Divining
Seeing and sharing a fuller picture of the past, present, and future

3. Synergizing
Understanding Self, Other, and We

4. Both/And-ing
Problem Solving from a mindset that assumes both are needed for success

Figure 1.3

When groups are able to dialogue and integrate both sides, they begin Synergizing and better understand that the polarity perspective allows for greater possibilities than either of the competing perspectives on their own. People realize that both perspectives are necessary if they want success to occur over time and begin to think from more of a Both/And perspective. They search beyond "my view versus your view" to find a more sustainable Third Way.

Not surprisingly, not only do groups who are able to Navigate Paradox end up with a more robust and sustainable solution to the issue, but they also experience positive results in the four areas that are negatively impacted when Suffering Paradox—communication, morale, results, and relationships. This is the real power of a polarity mindset that we'll explore and provide examples of throughout this book and series.

Because the group has harnessed the tension and turned it creative, a virtuous cycle is begun. The system can begin to experience the benefits of both poles, leading to higher morale and commitment. The trust and respect built during the process deepens communication and relationships, which can lead to better results in areas that have nothing to do with the polarity at hand and make the system more prepared to quickly solve problems in the future with less turmoil.

This is vital because polarities are everywhere. When we don't take the time, or know how, to deal with them, we can end up suffering—as individuals, in our relationships, as teams and organizations, and in societies. The good news is that making them object and navigating them effectively is possible with a proper sensemaking tool. The rest of this book, and this series, explores polarities and one such tool as a way to help people harness the power of polarities and help people navigate, not suffer, paradox.

In Summary:

- A polarity is a situation in which two interdependent and seemingly contradictory states must be maintained for success over time.

- Polarities require us to use both/and thinking, which is as important as either/or thinking but not more important.

- The point of polarities is not to swing between the poles but to find a way to harness the benefits of both poles.

- Both/and thinking doesn't come naturally, and many people find it helpful to have a tool to make the polarity object so that they have it, it doesn't have them.

- Navigating polarities leads to better results, higher morale, improved communication, and stronger relationships.

CHAPTER 2

HOW POLARITIES WORK

The good news about polarities is that they all work the same way. They follow a basic pattern and a set of rules that make it possible for us to not just understand them but to navigate them and leverage their inherent tension for good. And once we understand them, we can help others do the same and drive conversations that ease the suffering of paradox.

Chapter 3 outlines how to do that in a formulaic step-by-step fashion, but before getting there, we'll first examine how polarities work and some of the predictable elements of interdependent pairs.

There Is a Formula

Polarities are completely predictable and follow a basic pattern of behavior — a formula, if you will. Once we look at a polarity through this lens, it becomes easy to see the paradoxical dynamic more fully and act in ways that harness the creative tension available in all interdependent pairs.

The formula is simple and is easily demonstrated by Johnson's example of the dynamic of Inhale and Exhale.[1] Both of these poles are necessary for life, and doing each of them feels good in its own unique way. But doing one for too long while ignoring the other leads to a bad situation. Just try inhaling consistently without exhaling for a minute or two to see what we mean. To break the formula down, refer to Figure 2.1 on the following page.

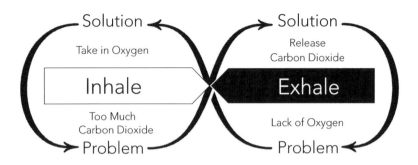

Figure 2.1: Inhale::Exhale

When we inhale, the lungs fill with air and we feel good and expansive as the body takes advantage of the oxygen. But as we inhale, the body takes the oxygen and turns it into carbon dioxide (CO_2), which is poisonous to the human system. If we keep inhaling and ignore the Exhale pole, we end up with too much CO_2 in our body, becoming constricted and light-headed, which is a problem. The good stuff (plenty of oxygen) becomes bad stuff (too much CO_2), and we experience the *overuses* of that pole. This leaves us in a predicament because the pole that we thought was such a good thing no longer seems so appealing.

When we have too much CO_2 in our system, there is only one logical solution to the problem, and that is to exhale. In the short term this feels really good and makes it seem as if we have solved our problem (we've gotten rid of all that CO_2). But if we hang out on this new pole and forget the pole we came from, before we know it, we sink to the new overuses and have another problem on our hands that seems to have one logical and obvious solution. We don't have enough oxygen, so we swing back to the original pole—Inhale! And so, the cycle goes.

This is how all polarities work. When we focus on a pole, we get lots of good things in the short term, which we call benefits. But if we focus our attention there too long and ignore the other pole, the positive state created by the benefits turns bad and we get the overuses of that pole. When this happens, the logical solution is to reach out for the other pole and to the benefits it promises. In the short term, the new benefits seem like a great solution and we're happy we made the switch. But as we begin to embrace the new pole more tightly, as if it were the only solution, the new benefits turn to overuses, which can drive us to swing back toward the original pole.

Energy Like the Infinity Loop (and not)

This dynamic of polarities is often represented by an infinity loop that demonstrates the natural flow of energy within and between the interdependent pair. The energy goes from the overuses of one pole to the benefits of the other, followed by a pull back toward the original pole as a result of anticipating or experiencing the overuses of the new pole. The arrows on the infinity loop represent this movement and serve as a reminder that the polarity is filled with energy—energy that can either turn destructive or be harnessed for creativity and power. It also demonstrates that the poles are connected *and* distinct entities. They are separated and kept apart as the loop crosses between them, AND they are one integrated pair, held together by the outside parts of the loop that wrap around them and pull them together.

A limitation of using the infinity loop in relation to polarities is that some mistake it as a suggestion that the answer is to swing between the poles like a pendulum. This is not the case. Think of organizations that oscillate between Centralized and Decentralized every few years as new leaders come and go. Swinging wastes resources and erodes the credibility of leaders. The bigger the swing, the bigger the waste and the higher the likelihood that the change won't succeed. The infinity loop is a reminder of the dynamic, of the energy flow. It is not a suggestion that the ideal state is to swing between the poles. Navigating polarities involves harnessing the benefits of both poles while excluding neither, a concept the infinity loop does not capture.

The way to remedy the swing from one pole to the other is to find what Richard Rohr[2] refers to as the Third Way — a state that overcomes the contradiction of the two parts to find a reconciling third force that is bigger than either pole yet excludes neither of them. To navigate polarities, it is helpful to first differentiate the poles, to pull them apart and understand the benefits and overuses of each. But then we must reintegrate the poles by identifying the Third Way that occurs when harmonizing the tension. Identifying actions that lead to the Third Way prevents a swing between poles. This harmonization — having both poles ring simultaneously — creates the point from which real leverage can occur and exceeds the benefits of balancing or equalizing, which are suboptimal goals. Leveraging the natural tension between the two poles and having the courage to step in to the Third Way allows us to harness the real power of the polarity.

For example, the braiding, or harmonization, of Inhale and Exhale in the example above is Breath. Breath is the Third Way that is bigger than both poles and honors both. When we can stand in the Third Way of a polarity, we move beyond either/or into a space of possibility and power. Our effectiveness skyrockets and our impact soars.

Benefits and Overuses

Each pole has a distinct set of benefits and overuses. The benefits are the upsides gained by focusing on that particular pole. They are the unique qualities a pole brings to the system and the reason that people value it or want to focus on it. They are the good that occurs as a result of embracing that pole. In Structure::Flexibility, focusing on Structure produces the benefits of predictability and control (to name a few). There are people who value these benefits and are therefore interested in pursuing Structure.

However, each pole also has overuses that occur as a result of over-focusing on that pole. They are the bad things that occur when there is *too much* of the pole. They are the negative impacts that can occur if there is an excess of the pole in the system. These overuses are *not* bad things about the pole—they are not a list of "cons." Nor are they the effects of using the pole poorly. Overuses are simply the result of too much focus on one pole or a neglect of the other.

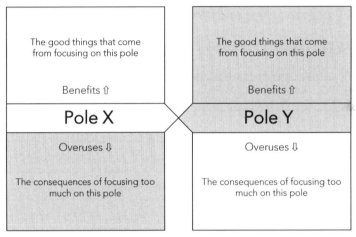

The good things that come from focusing on this pole

Benefits ⇧

Pole X

Overuses ⇩

The consequences of focusing too much on this pole

The good things that come from focusing on this pole

Benefits ⇧

Pole Y

Overuses ⇩

The consequences of focusing too much on this pole

Figure 2.2: Benefits and Overuses

This is an important distinction. In a polarity, there is nothing bad about either pole. For example, there is nothing bad about Candor—there are only downsides to overusing or having *too much* Candor. There are no cons to Collaboration, but bad things can happen when we overuse, or have *too much,* Collaboration. In the example of Structure::Flexibility above, there are no bad things about Structure. However, bad things such as rigidity and inflexibility can occur from the *overuse* of Structure. With an either/or mindset, it is tempting to make one of the poles "wrong" or "bad." This is part of what drives the phenomenon of Suffering Paradox. A both/and mindset sees nothing bad about either pole, only potential overuses, because the poles actually need each other to exist.

Need Each Other over Time

A foundational concept of polarities is that both poles need each other over time. They are not problems to be solved, but a relationship to be navigated. Continuing with the Structure::Flexibility example, Structure and Flexibility might seem like opposites to some, but they are actually interdependent. They are two sides of the same coin that depend on each other to exist. It's a bit of a mind twist, but if we didn't have Structure in the world, there would be no such thing as Flexibility. Over time, for success to occur, Structure actually needs Flexibility to save it from itself. And vice versa.

We need to find solutions that embrace both poles of a polarity, a Third Way, which requires us to supplement either/or thinking with both/and thinking. Both/and thinking allows us to address inherent interdependency and tension in order to maximize the potential of polarities.

Two Problems and Two Solutions

The fact that the poles need each other, and that neither one is wrong or has cons, doesn't mean that overuses aren't problematic. Overuses are painful things happening as a result of over-focusing on a pole and are typically experienced as problems. Naturally, as in any problematic situation, there is a desire to get rid of the pain by solving the issue. As illustrated by Figure 2.1 – Inhale::Exhale [page 26], the logical solution to the problem created by overuses always lies in the benefits of the other pole.

Seeing the situation from this diagonal – the benefits of one pole as the solution to the problems created by the overuses of the other pole – is one perspective. While this diagonal is technically accurate, it is unsustainable. Moving from the overuses of one pole to the benefits of the other pole may be a necessary correction but, alone, it is not a lasting solution because, over time, the problem-solution dynamic is happening on both sides of the polarity.

While this seems obvious and unproblematic on paper, it creates real hardship in groups and organizations in which one group of people sees one problem and pushes diagonally to the obvious solution while another group sees another problem and pushes along their diagonal toward their solution. Naturally, the conflict between these two perspectives creates tension and, as a result, the group Suffers Paradox as they work to prove their rightness. As Johnson is fond of saying, both of the perspectives are accurate, but neither is complete. However, by using a polarity lens and viewing the situation as an interdependent pair, people start to realize that there is yet a third perspective that respects and holds both of the first two simultaneously. The Third Way.

The Third Way

While Rohr discusses the concept of the Third Way from a spiritual perspective, the tenets translate directly to the organizational, leadership, and human levels. The Third Way is the space that reintegrates and braids the poles together. It is as if each pole is its own distinct musical note that the Third Way brings together in harmonization to create a new, unique tone that still contains both of the originals. They are both there, and yet, they are not. The Third Way is a more expansive way because it combines both of the parts while excluding neither of them, like the example of Breath above.

Standing in the Third Way is a commitment—to personal development, to growth, and to being with the truth of the interdependent relationship. We have to develop the mental clarity, emotional stability, and embodied presence to not be swept up in the natural cycle of the infinity loop—the ups and downs, values and fears. When we can do that, we step into a mindset and way of being that is fluid, not fixed, trusting, adaptable, and responsive.[3] The Third Way is a place of trust, courage, and love. It is from this sacred ground of seeing, accepting, and experiencing the interdependent nature of the dynamic that we are moved by, and to, a different energy. No longer are we pushed or pulled; no longer do we feel the need to choose one or the other; no longer do we identify who we are by our preferred pole. As we reconcile these seemingly opposite forces and we allow them to be harmonized within ourselves, we are moved by the extraordinarily simple and subtle force of the Third Way.

They All Work the Same Way — Work::Rest

To explore these concepts further, we'll examine several other polarities below. The first is the common example of Work and Rest, which is a basic building block of life and plays out in all levels of systems. Popularized by Johnson,[4] it demonstrates how polarities work and, because everyone can easily understand this dynamic, it's a great example to use when first explaining the concept of polarities to someone. Following this example are several other polarities with some of their benefits and overuses. As a practice, think of one or two benefits and overuses you'd add to both poles for each pair.

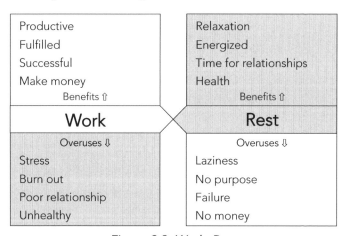

Figure 2.3: Work::Rest

In examining the map of Work::Rest, you no doubt noticed that the polarity follows the same pattern outlined for Inhale::Exhale above.

1. If an individual focuses on one pole (Work), they will experience the benefits of the pole on which they focus (productive, successful, and make money).

2. If that individual does not focus attention on the other pole (Rest), they will soon experience the overuses of the pole on which they are focusing (stress, burn out, and perhaps sickness).

3. When this happens, the solution to "the problem" seems to become one or more of the benefits of the other pole (relaxation, time for relationships, and health), which creates the attraction and energy to generate the movement toward the other pole.

4. However, the other pole is only part of the answer. If the individual continues to over-focus on the new pole (Rest) to the exclusion of the other (Work), they will then start to experience the overuses of that pole (laziness, failure, no money), which then increases the attraction to the upsides of the other pole.

This fundamental dynamic works the same way for all polarities.

The following page contains several polarities to practice with. Several benefits and overuses have been added to each. Take a second and add to the lists.

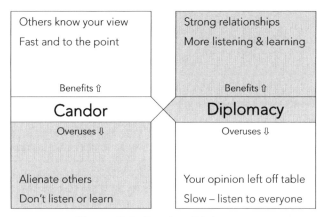

Figure 2.4: Candor::Diplomacy

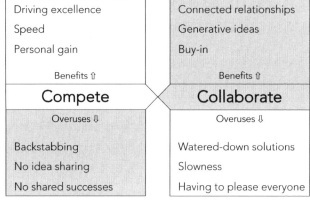

Figure 2.5: Compete::Collaborate

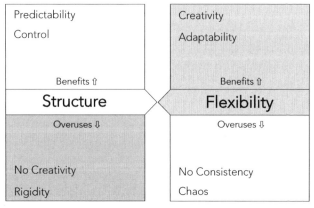

Figure 2.6: Structure::Flexibility

The Formula, Expanded

Before moving into the discussion about "what do we do about these things?" and "how do we leverage the dynamic once we see it?," it's helpful to first dig a little deeper into some of the inner workings of the polarity dynamic. Below are several key points with two examples threaded throughout. Again, these principles apply to all interdependent pairs.

Diagonals and Preferences

There are at least three different perspectives in any polarity, and we typically have a preference for one of them based on the pole we prefer. Our fondness might be slight or it might be strong, but we typically feel more comfortable embracing one of the two poles. Of course, we know both are important (hopefully) and wouldn't say that either one is (necessarily) bad, but when operating in default mode, we could pick one side of a center line to stand on.

When we prefer a pole, we value the benefits of that pole — they are the things that excite us, shape what we think is important in the world, motivate and drive our actions and decisions, and possibly define who we are. Conversely, we typically fear, or don't like, the overuses of the opposite pole. These things threaten the things we value, so therefore we will do whatever we can to move away from them or to make sure they don't happen. This sets up what we call a diagonal perspective.

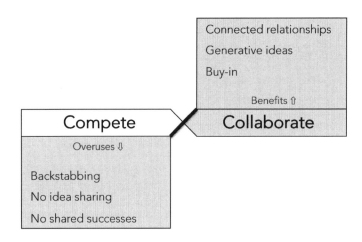

Figure 2.7: The Collaborate Diagonal

Using the image above, someone who holds the Collaborate diagonal values the benefits of collaboration—connected relationships, generative ideas, and buy-in. Likewise, they dislike or fear the overuses of Compete—backstabbing, no idea sharing, and no shared success. Seeing the world on this diagonal means they will likely spend a bit of energy figuring out how to move things *from* the overuses they fear *to* the benefits they value. This is one perspective.

A second perspective is the Compete diagonal. Individuals who hold this diagonal fear or dislike the overuses of Collaboration: slowness, a watered-down product, having to make everyone happy. Meanwhile, they value and love driving excellence, speed, and personal gain—the benefits of Compete. While both of these diagonal perspectives are accurate, neither is complete. Stepping off our diagonal and looking through a polarity lens allows us to see the situation more completely and to understand how the Third Way can benefit and enhance the things we value instead of threatening them.

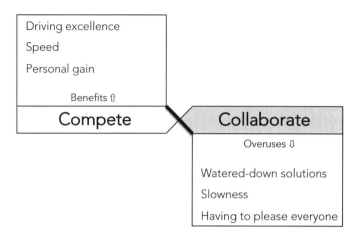

Figure 2.8: The Compete Diagonal

The More We Prefer, the More of Our Overuses We Tolerate

There is nothing inherently wrong about having a preference or holding a diagonal. The problem comes when the preference has us instead of us having it, and we begin to identify part of who we are by a diagonal. When that happens, and we get locked into our perspective, we can forget that, without the other pole, we won't be successful over time. When we prefer a pole and begin embracing it, we naturally begin to get the benefits and the things we value from that pole. Again, that's a good thing, there's nothing wrong with it. However, we can often become so enamored with those benefits — addicted even — that we don't realize we're slipping into the overuses. We learn to accept and endure the overuses and get fooled into thinking that "this is just the way things have to be for me to get (or be) the things I value." Ironically, as we experience more of these overuses, we actually begin to lose some of the benefits we wanted in the first place. This sets up a paradoxical dynamic in which to get more of the benefits of the pole we prefer, the solution isn't to hold onto it more tightly—the solution is to actually loosen our grip a bit to bring in more of the other pole.

Two Examples

These two points, and the ones that follow below, are easily demonstrated by two examples, one that refers back to the Work::Rest example in Figure 2.3 [page 32], and another that refers to Candor::Diplomacy in Figure 2.4 [page 34]. While obviously oversimplified and based on generalizations, the point is clear and serves as a good demonstration.

In the United States, as in many other societies, there is more of a preference for Work than Rest. If you read the things listed in the benefits of Work, they are, by and large, American values. They are things one is "supposed" to do if you are an American—be productive and personally fulfilled, make money, and get lots of recognition. Not that Americans think relaxation, time for relationships, and good health are unimportant, but there is more of a value placed on the benefits of Work.

The same could be said of other cultures that prefer the Work pole, such as the UK, Germany, and Japan, while the opposite could be said of countries that have a preference toward the Rest pole. Cultures such as those in Spain, Sweden, and Greece[5] place a bit more of an emphasis on time for relaxation, relationships, and health. Those things are valued and drive the members of those societies, even though productivity, personal fulfillment, and making money are not deemed bad things to do. Having preferences is not a bad thing or something to be eliminated—as long as we have them and they don't have us.

Issues arise when we have a preference for a pole and hold onto it too tightly. If Americans place such a value on being productive, having personal fulfillment, and making money, then why do they have a country "filled" with people who are stressed out, burned out, and unhealthy? Those issues make complete sense when you consider that they are the result of over-focusing on the pole they love—the overuses of Work. Take innovation for example. Two overuses of the Work pole are exhaustion and, therefore, a lack of creativity. There is a lot of talk right now about America losing its innovative edge. There are very few organizations for which innovation is not a current buzzword, and it's nearly impossible to pick up a business magazine that doesn't mention it in some way. No wonder! When people are exhausted, with no space for creativity, they can't be innovative. The answer to the innovation problem won't come from people working harder. Part of it will come from us learning to find the Third Way of Work::Rest. Unfortunately, Americans, in general, value the Work pole so much, that they're willing to tolerate the downsides that come as a result of over-focusing on it because they think that they are the natural byproducts of being successful. It's an unsustainable model based on an either/ or mindset.

Another example is the Candor::Diplomacy polarity mapped in Figure 2.4 [page 34] in the practice section. Let's look at two clients, Rachel and Rajeev. Rachel values speed in conversations and having people know where she stands, which are the benefits of Candor. Because of these values, it's not surprising that Rachel says she is a candid person. Not that she thinks diplomacy is a bad thing, but her preference is clear—she happily holds the Candor diagonal. She values the benefits of Candor and doesn't like the overuses of Diplomacy, namely, having to slow the process to a halt as she listens, not speaking her mind, and trying to make everyone feel good.

Rajeev, on the other hand, holds the Diplomacy diagonal. He values the benefits of Diplomacy, spending time learning from all points of view and having strong relationships. And he fears the overuses of Candor: being alienated and hurting people's feelings. Both Rajeev and Rachel have a preference for one of the poles and value the benefits that pole brings, which pushes them to see the world from a particular diagonal.

Additionally, because of the value they place on their respective poles, both Rachel and Rajeev are willing to tolerate some of the downsides that come with over-focusing on that pole. When asked, Rajeev will lament that he sometimes feels his voice doesn't get heard, he doesn't get his way, and he spends too much time seeking out other people's opinions, but he'll say that it's just the price he has to pay in order to get things done. Rachel, on the other hand, has received feedback that she sometimes alienates people and that they don't feel heard in conversations. While she's not particularly happy about it, she explains that sometimes that's the way it has to be because letting people know where one stands and moving things along quickly is so important. The more we prefer a pole, the more willing we are to tolerate the impact of its overuses and miss the fact that we may be losing some of the benefits we hoped to gain. In Rachel's case, one of her values is to let people know where she stands. However, because of her overuse, they've stopped listening and don't care where she stands!

The Deeper We Are, the Stronger the Pull

Another tenet of polarities is that the more we experience the overuses of a pole, the stronger the attraction to the benefits of the other pole. Said differently, the deeper we get pulled into the downsides of a pole, the more attractive the opposite benefits become because they look more and more like the solution to what ails us. We are experiencing a problem, and the bigger that problem becomes, the more we want to reduce our pain by moving toward the logical and obvious solution. The further we are in the overuses, the stronger the attraction to the opposite benefits, and the greater the risk we will default to an either/or mindset.

When Viewed Through its Overuses, Any Pole Looks Wrong

When we experience the problems that come from the overuses of a pole, it can be tempting to view the current circumstances and what led us there as a mistake. It is a logical reaction—we are experiencing a problem, so a natural response is to determine what caused the difficulty. People think, "Now look where we are. We should have never decentralized!" (or been so empowering or collaborative or structured—you fill in the pole). This increases the push toward the opposite pole as we try to get away from the "mistake" that's been made.

If not viewed through a polarity lens, it's easy to miss that the overuses or "problems" being experienced are a result of embracing a pole that brought with it many benefits as well. People can then begin to vilify the over-focused pole which, in turn, creates conflict with those who strongly value that pole and the benefits it brings ("Decentralization is stupid," "Empowering people is a mistake," "Collaboration is deadly and bogs us down"). It can also cause internal conflict, as we'll see with Rachel below. When we experience the problems that come with overuse, it's important to remember that embracing the pole was not a mistake. The "mistake" was embracing one pole while neglecting the other pole over time.

The Examples, Revisited

Both of these tenets are easily demonstrated in the examples used above. Consider, again, the polarity of Work::Rest. Imagine you work on a team of people that agreed to take on an exciting eighteen-month project requiring long hours, lots of weekend work, and no vacation time. While everyone knew it would be a big lift, it seemed worth it because of the personal satisfaction and extra money it would bring to everyone on the team. After the first month or two, people might be experiencing some stress and tiredness but most likely could tolerate the situation.

However, after ten to twelve months with no downtime and no weekends, the team would probably be pretty deep in the overuses of Work. You, and others, would likely be stressed out, burning out, exhausted, and possibly have negative health consequences. At that point, the desire for and attraction to time off, relaxation, and time with loved ones would be incredibly intense—exponentially more than they were in month two. The deeper we are in the overuses, the stronger the attraction to the opposite benefits.

Additionally, it is totally within reason to suggest that in month twelve, when people are extremely stressed, burned out, and exhausted, that several (or all!) people might begin to think, "Taking on this project was a big mistake in the first place." The cost of being exhausted no longer seems worth it because they have lost sight of the benefits that the project brings. These people are then seen as complainers aiming to harm the team and its success. Reiterating the point above, when experiencing the overuses, the move to the current pole can seem like a mistake and framing it as such can create tension with those who value the current pole and the benefits it brings.

Let's go back to Rachel and Candor. When Rachel joins a new team, she demonstrates, as is true to her nature, a fondness for Candor to the neglect of Diplomacy. In her eager attempt to experience the values that come along with the benefits of Candor, she starts to experience some of the overuses. Some of her new teammates begin to whisper that she doesn't listen and doesn't care about people's feelings. In fact, Rachel herself notices that people seem to be avoiding her but decides not to think much of it. Suppose Rachel doesn't change her behavior, and perhaps worse, holds even more tightly to the Candor pole in order to prove she's right. Over time, she'd experience even more alienation, which might intensify her desire, or her boss' demand, for her to connect with the team and be in conversation about their ideas (the benefits of Diplomacy). However, she's unlikely to do those things because, in her mind, it would mean getting the overuses of the Diplomacy pole—slowing down her work and diluting her voice at the table. The deeper we are in the overuses of our pole, the stronger our attraction to the benefits of the other pole, but we're unlikely to reach for them because of our fear of the opposite overuses.

Now, assume that Rachel's boss pulls her aside and tells her the reason she isn't getting a promotion is because of her Candor—she doesn't listen to the input of others, damages relationships, and people don't enjoy working with her. In her anger over not getting the promotion, Rachel tells her friend, "Speaking my mind was a big mistake and, from now on, I'm not going to say anything! And I definitely won't give people my input!" As a result, she throws the baby out with the bathwater. She now sees Candor as a mistake and wants to avoid it instead of seeing that the real mistake was having too much Candor and neglecting Diplomacy.

It's Difficult to See and Stand in the Third Way

The logical question probably arising by now is, if the overuses are so bad, and if the opposite benefits are so attractive, what keeps us from shifting? Why don't we simply find ways to embrace more of the other pole and garner all of the upsides it brings? It seems so obvious. Unfortunately, it's a bit more complicated than it appears.

Stepping off our diagonal and into the Third Way can be tough and scary for several reasons. First, there is a legitimate fear of losing the things we value (the benefits of our preferred pole). We would rather live with the downsides we're experiencing than risk giving them up. Second, stepping into the Third Way often challenges the way we assume the world works. Kegan and Lahey's[6] work on our immunity to change explores how difficult it is to challenge these types of assumptions.

Perhaps the scariest part of stepping off our diagonal is the fear of losing the things that define part of who we are. When a piece of our identity is attached to a diagonal and becomes threatened by another person or situation, the natural reaction is to fight and resist. The brain wants to protect its image of who we are, and the heart fears the perceived risk of standing in the Third Way.

Let's go back to Rajeev's love of Diplomacy and the value he places on relationships, listening, and learning from multiple points of view outlined in the polarity in Figure 2.4 [page 34]. In fact, these benefits are so important to him that Rajeev and others on the team identify him as "the relationship guy." As a result, Rajeev holds Diplomacy quite tightly and gets the over-uses of the very pole he loves. Rajeev has expressed a real desire to let people know where he stands and bring his ideas to table. He wants to make changes, but no matter how attractive the benefits of Candor seem, he hesitates to embrace more of the pole.

In Rajeev's mind (but maybe not in actuality), he has to give up an essential piece of his identity—the warmth he brings to his relationships—in order to bring more Candor to the situation. This takes us back to the brain's propensity for either/or thinking. He is also reluctant to be more candid for the fear that he will hurt people's feelings (the overuses of Candor). For Rajeev, the possibility of either of those becoming true is far worse than his voice and ideas not being heard (the overuses of Diplomacy).

When we step into the Third Way, we are being asked to expand rather than shed. But the habitual nature of either/or thinking coupled with the fear of loss and the fear of potential pain are so scary (probably subconsciously) that it doesn't feel that way. It keeps Rajeev from loosening his grip on Diplomacy so he can also hold onto the benefits of Candor. His either/or mindset makes it seem like he has to shed a part of who he is, when in reality a both/and mindset calls him to *expand* who he is. It's difficult for Rajeev to wrap his mind around this, and it feels risky and uncomfortable. Simply stated, when the mind can't resolve it and the heart can't make space for it, either/or becomes an attractive solution. That, coupled with our discomfort of discomfort, makes standing in the Third Way a challenge.

Understanding the discomfort of perceived loss, the uncertainty of what might happen when we loosen our grip around our preferred pole, and the vulnerability of risking part of who we understand ourselves to be are all a part of navigating polarities. Although fear, vulnerability, and grief are part of the common ground of humanity, they are ground we aren't always taught how to stand on. If you think about it, many of us have organized our entire lives around not feeling losses that have already happened and protecting ourselves against future loss. So it's no surprise that seeing and standing in the Third Way can seem difficult. When we operate with an either/or mindset, we believe we must give up the benefits of our preferred pole (Rajeev's value for listening and learning) and lose the thing that has served us so well (Rajeev is "the relationship guy"). The brain's mastery and circuitry for either/or thinking means that we must develop self-awareness and work harder to navigate the world with a both/and mindset.

Navigating Requires Vulnerability

Navigating polarities and standing in the Third Way can require vulnerability and working with uncomfortable emotions like anxiety, fear, and grief, topics generally overlooked by other approaches aimed at helping people make sense of paradox. Brené Brown[7] talks about the correlation between our ability to stand in the "tension of the and," or the Third Way, and our capacity for discomfort. She suggests our need for either/or is driven by our fear of the vulnerability required by both/and, outlined above. The shift from Suffering Paradox to Navigating Paradox, therefore, requires us to expand our emotional capacity for discomfort and risk, which can make embracing a both/ and mindset trickier and more involved than it appears on the surface.

At this point, many people ask what vulnerability sounds and looks like when we are standing in the "tension of the and" and in the midst of Navigating Paradox. Let's turn back to Rajeev's love of Diplomacy and his desire to bring more Candor to his relationships. As a reminder, Rajeev expressed a real longing to let people know where he stands and to bring his ideas to the table. He really wants to make changes, but no matter how attractive the benefits of Candor seem, he hesitates to embrace more of the pole. As Rajeev considers bringing more Candor to his conversations, he often says, "I'm known for my diplomatic approach to work and relationships. It's why people come to me for solutions and advice. I can't give that up." That is the voice of vulnerability. That is what's at risk for Rajeev — people may stop coming to him. That is the emotional exposure and discomfort that lives at the heart of Navigating Paradox.

In other situations, it might sound like this:

- If I give them more flexibility, I might get taken advantage of.
- People will think I'm weak if I don't move fast and make a decision.
- We could miss our short-term sales targets by being more collaborative.
- I'd be bored stiff and feel confined if we implement too many processes.
- My team would think I'm a sellout if I started collaborating across the organization.

Like Rajeev, what many of us want to do in these situations is pull away from the discomfort and run from the resistance. We react to the brain's impulse and craving for predictability. We fight the fear and flee from the discomfort to once again feel the safety, coziness, and perceived certainty of our preferred pole. While staying in the safety of our diagonal may seem comfortable, it is seriously detrimental to our individual and collective potential. When we do this, we can never stand in the Third Way and therefore never harness all of the power that comes from navigating the polarity well.

Standing in the Third Way takes practice. Standing in the Third Way *is* a practice. It relies on a way of being and doing that most of us were never taught. It requires that we pause and look inward to discover how old habits and hidden assumptions undermine the results we seek. It requires self-awareness, conscious choice, and courageous action. This is why a sensemaking tool like the Navigator is so important.

When we find the capacity to be honest with ourselves and others, we can start to move into a true sense of harmonization. When we move toward vulnerability with awareness and make space for what is, the fear can relax, and our hearts can open even more to the contradiction of the "and." As Parker Palmer[8] says, it is the mind that pushes us to either/or, and it is only in the heart that we can resolve the contradictions.

Seeing More Completely and Driving Different Conversations

To close this chapter, it is worth mentioning a few of the ways navigating the polarity dynamic can positively impact our lives, our organizations, and the world.

A Richer Perspective

As highlighted above, each polarity contains two sets of problems and two sets of solutions. This sets up a situation in which all polarities contain two distinct points of view, or diagonals. Conflicts between differing points of view are the source of much negative tension in groups, organizations, and society. Without a constructive way to make sense of it, the tension can become chronic and have serious impacts as things get personal with neither party having anything constructive to say about the other. Take many of the world's political situations as a case in point.

Knowing about polarities and how they work allows us to move beyond just our perspective and helps us to see the world more richly. Helping people make sense of polarities by helping to make them object allows people to navigate the situation differently and thereby see and connect to the world more fully. We agree with the research by Brené Brown[9] that suggests this is what the world is hungry for. When we are able to be vulnerable and courageously step off our diagonal to look for the Third Way, we can't help but see and connect to ourselves, the world, and the people in it more fully.

Seeing Others More Fully

Another drawback of seeing the world on diagonals is that it limits how we see others. When we have a preference for a pole and hold a particular point of view, we tend to see those who prefer the other pole in terms of its overuses not its benefits. We simplify and segment how we see them and can get trapped in what Jennifer Garvey Berger[10] calls simple stories. We don't see them fully, which inhibits our ability to understand their point of view. This makes it easy to paint them as the villain in our story instead of the hero in theirs. Here's an example that builds on the Compete::Collaborate map from earlier in the chapter in Figure 2.5 [page 34].

In an organization with regional sales teams, there were two leaders who constantly butted heads and who grew increasingly annoyed with one another. When each was asked about the other, neither had many, if any, positive comments about the other. Antonio said that Erica and her team never shared ideas, were worried only about their own goals, and were a bunch of back-stabbers. Unfortunately, Erica's view of Antonio wasn't much better. She claimed his team was too slow and, in trying to involve everyone, they always ended up with watered-down ideas.

Erica and Antonio were often stuck and at odds because they held two different diagonals and, as a result, saw the world, and each other, very differently. Erica had a preference for competition, while Antonio preferred collaboration. Erica valued the benefits of Compete and loathed the overuses of Collaborate. Looking from her diagonal, she couldn't see the benefits that Antonio (and his pole) brought, she could only see him in terms of the overuses (i.e., slow, watered-down ideas). The same was true on the other side of the equation. Antonio could only see Erica through the lens of how she threatened the very things that Antonio held dear. Her pole's overuses threatened Antonio's values, and thus, he could only see Erica through that lens.

This is true in other polarities as well. We often view those who hold our point of view in terms of their benefits and those who prefer the other pole in terms of their overuses. It's tempting and easy for us to see how "they" get in our way, how "they" make situations a bit more difficult, how "they" are leading us on a path of destruction. We don't typically stop to say, "Wow, look at the upsides and gifts this person brings to the situation!"

Viewing situations and people through a polarity lens allows us to see other people more completely. We see they hold a per-spective that is interdependent, not contradictory, to ours — and that sustained success requires both of our perspectives. Instead of seeing them from our diagonal, we can step back and see them more fully, which can only bring good things to the world because, as Barry Johnson says, the more fully we see someone, the harder it is not to love them.

In the end, our hope is to increase our individual and collective capacity for appreciating and understanding different perspectives, and our goal is to help people make sense of polarities so they can drive different conversations in their families, teams, communities, organizations, societies, and the world. The process is not difficult if we have a sensemaking tool that helps people make the polarities in their lives object. The next chapters outline the process of using one such tool, the Polarity Navigator, to help people find the Third Way in order to successfully Navigate Paradox.

In Summary:

- We often have a preference for one pole over the other.
- Our preferences and our fears can drive us to see the world on diagonals.
- The stronger our preference for a pole, the more we will tolerate its overuses.
- The deeper we are in the overuse, the stronger the attraction to the opposite benefits.
- When experiencing the overuse of a pole, that pole looks like a mistake.
- Our attachment to our diagonal means we sometimes need help seeing the Transformational Third Way.
- Navigating the Third Way requires vulnerability—stepping into it can feel risky.
- The more we preference a pole, the more likely we are to define some part of our identity by that pole and the more vulnerability it takes to step toward the Third Way.
- Our fear of the opposite downsides and/or losing part of our identity keeps us from both/and.
- Both/and is unresolvable by just the mind. It is a job for the heart.

CHAPTER 3

USING THE POLARITY NAVIGATOR TO MAP POLARITIES

This chapter is a step-by-step approach to creating a Polarity Navigator, a mapping tool that helps people make sense of interdependent pairs and identify ways to navigate them in their lives. The tool is both simple and complex and can be used at any level of system—individual, team, family, organization, community, or society. This chapter outlines the basic steps of creating a Polarity Navigator. Chapter 4 discusses how this mapping process fits into a larger formula for using polarities within a system and provides several high-level case examples.

Background of the Polarity Navigator

The Polarity Navigator stands firmly on the shoulders of the work of Barry Johnson and the contributions that he and the entire community of polarity practitioners have made to helping people understand interdependent pairs. Additionally, the Navigator builds on Johnson's sensemaking map by incorporating not only the elements we often find our clients need to successfully navigate polarities, but also the thinking of Richard Rohr, Parker Palmer, Brené Brown, and Smith and Lewis. The combination of these elements has been highlighted throughout this book and will be expounded on below, but in short, the Polarity Navigator helps people make sense of polarities by allowing them to:

- Differentiate the Poles—to fully understand the interdependent pair, we have to be able to pull the poles apart and understand the benefits and overuses of each.
- Reintegrate the Poles—to be able to leverage the dynamic,

we have to have a way to braid the poles back together and
identify the Transformational Third Way.

• Name the Vulnerability—standing in the Third Way often
challenges how we see the world and ourselves in it, which
requires vulnerability.

• Integrate Action Steps—the point of making sense is to
take action, so it is vital to clearly identify and capture
strategies for navigating the polarity from the Third Way.

The Navigator as a Sensemaking Map

According to Stigliani and Ravasi,[1] when dealing with particularly complex circumstances, effective individuals and groups
rely on visual maps to make sense and take action. Using a map
gives people a way to organize complex ideas and to make object
things they might otherwise be subject to. In the realm of polarities, this allows people to better understand interdependent pairs
and develop what Smith and Lewis[2] call a paradox cognition—a
key element of successfully dealing with paradox in the world.

The Polarity Navigator meets all six of Huff and Jenkins'[3]
requirements for a tool to be an effective sensemaking map in
complex situations. It is (a) a visual model that (b) lays out a
territory and (c) gives language to the things that make up the territory while (d) placing those things in at least two relationships
simultaneously. It also allows (e) individuals to place themselves
within the mapped domain and (f) make mental movement
throughout the territories that compose the map. In short, a good
map of a polarity helps people more fully see the polarity and,
thereby, have it instead of it having them.

That said, it's important to remember that a map is just that, a
map. It is not the actual thing the map represents. A map flattens
the terrain so we can make sense of it more quickly and then take
appropriate action. It can never capture all of the nuances and

details of the thing it represents. The Navigator is no different. It flattens the polarity, which in actuality, is a dynamic entity that can't fully be captured on a two-dimensional map. After mapping, the key is to unleash the polarity and allow it to spring back to life.

Doing it Right::Just Doing It

A quick aside before we jump in. A polarity at play when approaching any new skill is Doing It Right::Just Doing It. One possible way to look at this polarity is shown in Figure 3.1.

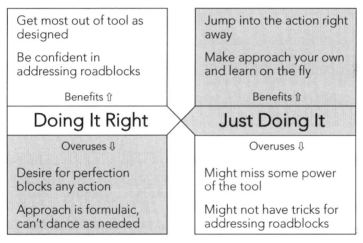

Get most out of tool as designed	Jump into the action right away
Be confident in addressing roadblocks	Make approach your own and learn on the fly
Benefits ⇧	Benefits ⇧
Doing It Right	**Just Doing It**
Overuses ⇩	Overuses ⇩
Desire for perfection blocks any action	Might miss some power of the tool
Approach is formulaic, can't dance as needed	Might not have tricks for addressing roadblocks

Figure 3.1: Doing It Right::Just Doing It

As you read this chapter and start to use the Navigator, we encourage you to keep this polarity in mind. Which of the poles is your preference—what's your diagonal? In what ways have you gotten the benefits and/or overuses of that pole when learning other new skills? What might be gained by bringing more of the other pole into your style?

One thing is certain. You cannot mess this up. While there *are* techniques that help create stronger maps with more impactful actions, any attempt to step back and make sense of a polarity with a mapping tool is better than plunging full force ahead without one.

The Mapping Process

A Polarity Navigator and a short description of each of its parts is shown in Figure 3.2 on the following page. The sections below describe the process for completing each portion of the Navigator in a somewhat formulaic order. While this is the process typically followed, there are many instances where the completion of the map happens in a different order, with steps often revisited for clarification and further understanding. Regardless of the process you follow, the involvement of stakeholders in every step is helpful, and often critical, for success.

Stakeholders

A crucial consideration when understanding a polarity is the involvement of key stakeholders. In a best-case scenario, key stakeholders would be involved in all aspects of creating the Navigator, or at least the benefits and overuses of each pole. One benefit of a Polarity Navigator is that it allows us to see the interdependent pair and its dynamic more fully. Stakeholders help this process by shedding light on our blind spots. And because some stakeholders will have a preference for our less-preferred pole, involving them in the mapping process allows us to see and better understand their perspective, enabling us to tap into the wisdom of any resistance they might have.

If it's not possible to involve stakeholders in the creation of the actual map, find other ways to include their perspective. Sit and share a draft of the Navigator to get feedback and input on the thinking that went into it. Seek to understand how they see the benefits and overuses of the polarity and check if the strategies you are considering will actually allow you all to stand in the Third Way. Regardless of how you do it, make stakeholder involvement a priority as you begin the mapping process.

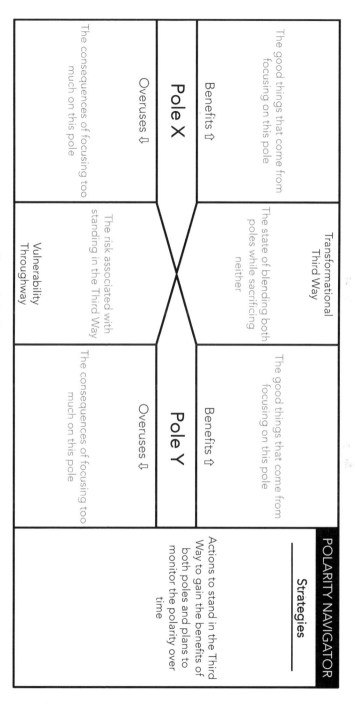

Figure 3.2: The Polarity Navigator

The Process

There are five key areas of focus when completing the Polarity Navigator. Each step is described in more detail below followed by a simple case example. Questions for completing each step of the process are outlined in Figure 3.12 [page 90] at the end of this chapter. The key components of the Navigator are:

1. Pole Names—Create names for each of the poles.

2. Benefits and Overuses—Differentiate the poles by identifying the good things the pole brings as well as the problems that arise when there is too much of it.

3. The Transformational Third Way—Reintegrate the poles by identifying what they look like when harmonized.

4. The Vulnerability Throughway—Identify the risks and courage needed to step into the tension that creates the Third Way.

5. Strategies—Brainstorm and decide on actions to navigate the polarity from the Third Way over time.

While these steps are laid out sequentially, in actuality, the process can be less so. Revisiting earlier steps is often helpful to more fully understand the polarity. The only caution is to resist jumping to strategies too quickly—be sure to build awareness before moving to action.

Step One—Pole Names

The names of the poles go in the pointed arrow boxes along the middle of the map. These boxes meet at the point where the infinity loop crosses as a reminder that the polarity dynamic consists of two poles (e.g., Structure and Flexibility) while simultaneously being just one entity (e.g., Structure::Flexibility).

If you have already identified the polarity you want to map, this is an easy step—there are many polarities listed throughout the book and in Appendix A - Lists of Polarities [page 157].

However, seeing and naming a polarity at play in a situation can be a bit tricky. Chapter 5 is dedicated solely to this topic. Regardless of how the polarity is identified, here are several things that can be helpful when naming the poles.

Tips for Creating Pole Names

Neutral Names

The most critical part of naming the poles is to ensure that both terms are neutral and not value laden. People are often tempted to name a pole by using one of its benefits, or worse, one of its overuses. For example, creating a map of Stability::Change yields different results than one that examines Stability and Chaos! Similarly, in a hospital, Focus on Patient Health and Capitalism would better be named Focus on Patient Health::Focus on Fiscal Health. It is important to equalize both poles to make it safe for all perspectives to be brought into the conversation and mapping process.

There are several questions you can ask to make pole names more neutral. If someone, or a group, has named a pole with one of its overuses, such as Stability and Chaos, questions like these can help find a neutral name:

- "Chaos" seems like it might be the result of having *too much* of something…what might that be?
- What is it that creates "Chaos" that, in some situations, might be an OK, or good, thing?
- "Chaos" is an interesting choice of words…How might someone who values the flip side of "Stability" name this pole?

It is also important to make sure that poles aren't named with one of their benefits. For example, instead of Candor::Diplomacy, someone may name a polarity Strong Leadership and Diplomacy. If so, asking questions like these can be helpful:

- What is the flip side of "Diplomacy" that makes for "Strong Leadership"?
- What is "Strong Leadership" the result of in this situation—it's because...?
- "Strong Leadership" sounds more like the benefit or byproduct of something...what might that be?

When creating a Navigator with a group, there will usually be people who value each of the poles. When this is the case, helping the group determine neutral pole names begins the process of having the two "sides" listen to one another and gain insight into the other's perspective. There are other ideas of how to work with groups in Chapter 4.

Clustering Names and Creating Keys

Do not let the pressure of coming up with the "right" name for a pole get in the way of creating a map. Often groups and individuals grind to a halt debating the name of the pole, saying things like, "It could be Structure...or Control...or even Processes...we can't decide." As long as the terms are neutral, it's best to pick one and go, then come back and modify as needed (remember, Do it Right::Just Do it).

Sometimes, though, it can be difficult to define a pole with, or come to agreement about, just one term. While not always ideal, it is possible to put several terms that describe a pole into one of the spaces on the Navigator. The caution here is to make sure you are not attempting to map several very different polarities at one time. If that's the case, it can be helpful to break them into separate Navigators to keep the conversation cleaner and more focused.

For example, using the hospital example above, it might be difficult to get people to agree to "Patient Health" as a pole name. Some might say "it's more about safety," while others say, "it's about wait times in the ER," and still others are saying, "it's quality of care." Again, while it's preferable to come to a concise name for the pole, in this instance, one could name one pole Focus on Safety/Quality/Health and the other Focus on Finances/Bottom-Line. While not a textbook way to create a Navigator, it works.

An alternate solution is to create a key to the map that defines a particular pole. Continuing with the example above, you could name the poles Care and Business with a key that outlines:

Care = Patient Safety, Quality of Care, Patient Satisfaction

Business = Strong Finances, Efficiencies, and Processes

As long as the terms are neutral and you aren't trying to deal with multiple polarities at once, these techniques can yield powerful maps that identify actions to navigate the polarity — which is, ultimately, the entire point.

Case Example:

The case running through this chapter draws on the example of Erica and Antonio in Chapter 2 [page 49].

Erica is a high achiever who received feedback from her manager that she needed to "stop being so competitive and form stronger relationships to increase your effectiveness." Perplexed about what that even meant, let alone how she would do it, she reached out to her coach, who opted to use the Navigator to help Erica explore the situation. After a short explanation of polarities and the Work::Rest example, they discussed how to name the polarity Erica was currently suffering.

When asked to name the poles, Erica's first suggestions were Competitive and Mediocrity—definitely not neutral names! So, the coach nudged her. "Mediocrity seems like it might be an overuse of something. What is it that, when taken too far, leads to mediocrity?" After some discussion, Erica identified that too much Collaboration could lead to mediocre or watered-down solutions, so she named the polarity Compete::Collaborate (see Figure 3.3 on the following page).

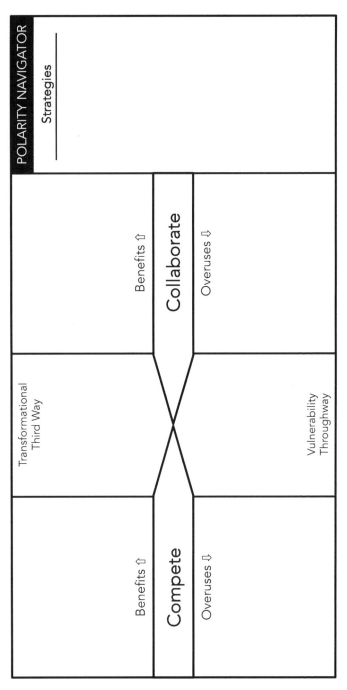

Figure 3.3: Compete::Collaborate

Step Two—Benefits and Overuses

Creating the benefits and overuses of the poles is a way to differentiate them from one another and allows people to see how both are needed for success over time. Chapter 4 has several considerations for facilitating this process with groups.

The benefits are the positive results that occur when focusing on a particular pole. These are written in the spaces above each pole name. While there are no minimum or maximum number of benefits for any polarity, you should aim for an equal number for each pole. Creating a Navigator that identifies fifteen benefits for Focus on Employees but only three for Focus on the Organization is obviously problematic and likely tells you a lot about the diagonals and preferences of those completing the Navigator!

When creating benefits, questions like these can be helpful:

• What benefits come from focusing on this pole?

• What are the positive results of holding this pole?

• If we could focus on this pole and not have to worry about the other, what good things would we get?

• What positive impacts does this pole have on the system/customers/employees/others?

• How does this pole contribute to overall success?

Overuses are the negative impacts that occur from the over-focus on, or having too much of, a pole. When a system, individual, or team does too much of a pole, problems arise. As with the benefits, aim for an equal number of overuses for each pole in order to show that each pole has an equal chance at eliciting downsides. Ideally, the number of overuses would be equal to the number of benefits.

When creating overuses, questions like these can be helpful:

• What happens when someone focuses only on this pole and neglects/ignores the other pole?

- If there is too much of this pole—if there isn't any/enough of the other pole—what results?
- What does it look like when this pole is taken too far, when we don't pay attention to the other side of the equation?
- How might too much of this pole impact the system/ customers/employees/other?
- How would an overuse of this pole detract from overall success?

When listing the benefits and overuses, or helping others create lists, it's important to remember that the benefits and over-uses are different than a list of pros and cons. In a polarity, there is nothing bad about either pole. There are no cons. When working with polarities, you may hear people starting to say things like, "the bad thing about Flexibility is…" There is nothing inherently bad about Flexibility, only bad things that happen from *too much* Flexibility. There are no cons to Decentralization, only negative impacts of *too much* Decentralization. This is an important distinction that can help lower resistance to change efforts and increase people's ability to appreciate the gifts of their less-preferred pole.

Tips for Creating Benefits and Overuses

Diagonals are Opposites

It has probably become obvious by now that the items in the quadrants on the diagonals of the Navigator are opposites. Said differently, the benefits of one pole are the opposite of the overuses of *the other* pole. These quadrants are connected by the diagonal lines in the center of the Navigator. Interestingly, the only opposites in a polarity are the diagonals. The poles of the polarity are not opposites—they are interdependent.

This is important because many times we have difficulty seeing the overuses of the pole we prefer and/or the benefits of the opposite pole. We are experts at seeing the benefits of the pole we prefer and the bad things (overuses) about the people who hold our less-preferred pole, but seeing our own overuses? Not so much. Using the diagonals as a resource can help us gain a fuller picture of the dynamic at play and to see the situation, and the people in it, more completely. While it can be tempting to simply fill out one quadrant and then transfer the opposites to the quadrant on the diagonal, it is best to spend time discussing and thinking about each quadrant in isolation of the other. Then, check the robustness of your Navigator by examining each item in a quadrant and ensuring that its opposite shows up in the diagonal quadrant. This can lead to different insights and understanding of the complete dynamic of the polarity.

Identical Upsides and Downsides Need "Because"

When an identical item shows up in more than one quadrant, it's important to put a "because" after it. Take Stability::Change, for example. In an organization, an overuse of Stability could be "Employee turnover." Likewise, "Employee turnover" could be an overuse of too much Change. Adding a "because" after each would provide a more robust picture of the polarity. An overuse of Stability could be "Employee turnover because people are bored," while for Change, the overuse would be "Employee turnover because of the constant chaos." The same could be true of the benefits. For Stability, "Employee satisfaction because there is a lack of surprises" and for Change, "Employee satisfaction because there are opportunities to learn new things." This increased detail makes it easier, and more likely, to develop effective strategies to navigate the polarity.

Use Nouns and Verbs

A common temptation is to list partial or incomplete thoughts in the overuses or benefits. There are many examples of this in this book — where we attempt to outline the benefits and overuses in a bulleted list of one or two words. While this can be helpful for speed and to give a general view of the dynamic at play in a polarity, it can make identifying the Third Way and creating strategies more difficult.

An alternative is to begin each upside or downside with a noun and a verb. Doing so makes it easier to identify what might be done to get those benefits and what the harmonization of them might look like. See Figure 3.4 for some examples. While perfect grammar isn't necessary, complete sentences make action planning much easier. Again, most groups don't start with this level of granularity—they will do generic benefits or overuses and then revisit the quadrants to flesh out the details.

Using Nouns and Verbs in Upsides and Downsides	
Less Actionable *Instead of listing...*	**More Actionable** *...try something like this.*
Timely	Customers are satisfied because of timely delivery
Listening	Employees feel heard and understood
Empowerment	Teams are empowered to make decisions
Information Sharing	Departments have insight into key projects of other departments

Figure 3.4: Using Nouns and Verbs in Upsides and Downsides

Order Doesn't Matter—Necessarily

There is no one best quadrant to begin the mapping process in, and no specific order for which quadrant should be filled out when. You can start anywhere, but most groups naturally default to following the path of the infinity loop. Any order is fine, and often you will want to bounce back and forth between quadrants as different items emerge.

That said, if a group is experiencing tension between subgroups that prefer different poles, it can be wise to start with the benefits of both poles before discussing the overuses of either. Additionally, it can be helpful (especially with overuses) to have the group identify just a few of the overuses of one pole and then flip to the other pole to identify several items before flipping back and forth between each pole. This keeps both camps engaged and helps to reduce tension that might be present.

Values Clarification

The process of determining benefits and overuses can often help people clarify their own values and better understand those of people who have a preference for the other pole. For example, in a group, someone might say that an overuse of Flexibility is "Frustration." In the discussion, someone else might say, "I disagree. Flexibility isn't frustrating." By using some of the questions listed below, the group can clarify that too much Flexibility might be frustrating because "people would change deadlines whenever they pleased," for example. Likewise, two people might disagree about whether "Strong Leadership" is a benefit of Candor. Through exploration, it might become clear that one person sees strong leadership as a byproduct of Candor because "people know where you stand and can trust what you say." This is something both parties can likely agree to as a positive result of Candor.

To help people reach agreement and better understand each other, you can ask the person whose ideas are being questioned for more clarification using inquiries such as:

- What about "Candor" leads to "Strong Leadership"?
- What is it about too much "Flexibility" that can be "Frustrating"?
- You said that "Satisfaction" is a benefit of "Focus on the Bottom Line" — why is that? What about this pole would create "Satisfaction"?

After the person answers, ask the person who initially disagreed whether or not the clarification makes sense. If so, add the clarification to the Navigator to create the fuller picture.

Case Example

To illustrate several of these points, let's go back to Erica and her coach. As they worked to identify the benefits and overuses of the Compete::Collaborate polarity (see Figure 3.5 [page 68]), the coach used several of the tips above to complete a more robust map.

- **Nouns and Verbs.** Initially, Erica identified "speed" as a benefit of Compete. Her coach asked, "What about speed? What's fast?" to which Erica replied, "People work fast because they don't want to get left behind." This built more awareness than simply capturing "speed" as a benefit.

- **Identical items need a "Because."** When identifying the benefits of Compete, Erica wrote, "Sr. Leadership is impressed." When she was writing the benefits of Collaborate, she put down, "Sr. Leadership is happy." The coach pointed out that the two items were virtually identical and therefore would benefit by putting a "because" after them that provided deeper insight into what things were important to Sr. Leaders.

- **Diagonals are Opposites.** As they were completing the process, Erica noticed that she had fewer things in the overuses of Compete than in the other boxes. (It's not unusual to see fewer overuses of the pole we prefer.) This prompted her to look at the items on the diagonal to see if she had captured everything. She realized the opposite of "We trade leads to drive business" was missing from the overuses of Compete, so made an addition (circled in Navigator, below). This really caught her attention and made her pay attention to the polarity in a different way.

- **Values Clarification.** Erica and the coach explored how the benefits of Compete were the things that Erica valued— they drove her actions and decisions on a regular basis. However, during the conversation, the coach pointed out that the items in the overuses of Collaborate were things that Erica had said when complaining about Antonio. "Yep, that pretty much describes him," Erica said with a snide look. "Is it possible that what he really wants is this," the coach asked while pointing to the benefits of Collaborate. Erica paused and they entered a rich conversation about the simple stories[4] she regularly created about Antonio's motivations.

Step Three—Transformational Third Way

The Transformational Third Way is the space on the Navigator that reintegrates the two poles after examining them separately. It is a space of experience, being, and heart where transformation is possible by harmonizing both poles.

It isn't a compromise, a back-and-forth, or something the two poles share in common. Rather, it captures what Rohr[5] refers to when speaking about the Third Way — it's a place where we can honor the difference between the poles, hold and reintegrate both, and eliminate neither. And it allows us to experience the power Palmer[6] alludes to when he suggests that if we can embrace the paradoxical tension, we can transform the inherent contradiction of a polarity into a creative and transformative force.

POLARITY NAVIGATOR	Strategies

Compete

Benefits ⇑
- We focus on excellence to win
- People work fast
- Individuals/I get big rewards
- We hit stretch targets
- Sr. Leadership is impressed because we exceed goals

Overuses ⇓
- Teams try to destroy each other
- We have blinders that limit ideas
- Others are resentful/don't buy in
- Teams get cut-throat and toxic
- People don't share leads or info which limits business revenue

Transformational Third Way

Vulnerability Throughway

Collaborate

Benefits ⇑
- I develop deeper relationships
- We create synergy of ideas
- Others buy in to our solutions
- We trade leads to drive business
- Sr. Leadership is happy because there is better morale

Overuses ⇓
- We focus on feelings, not success
- We involve everyone – it's slow
- Rewards are shared, no incentive
- Results and people are mediocre
- We miss strategic goals

Figure 3.5: Compete::Collaborate Benefits and Overuses

Tips for Discovering the Transformational Third Way

You Can't Think Your Way Through It

The Transformational Third Way invites us to step into a whole different type of knowing. It requires us to "get out of our head" and the endless stream of beliefs, opinions, and points of view that justify our either/or mindset. The Third Way requires a more intuitive way of knowing to experience the reality of being with both "this" and "that." This is something Adyashanti[7] says takes great subtlety, an ability to keep it simple, and a willingness to go beyond all of our notions—even our notions of right and wrong.

Part of this relates back to the nut and bolt example and the fact that not having language to express the combination or harmonization of two seemingly contradictory states can make articulating, and even seeing, the Third Way a challenge. Given that, it is useful to think about this part of the Navigator as a place to capture *experience*, not logic or actions.

Naming the Third Way

Naming is important. When we name something, we can see it more clearly and can then aim for it as a state of being. This can be a tricky step in the Navigator.

To articulate the experience of having both "this" and "that" — what it would *be* like—it can be helpful to use metaphors or to create original names or concepts. These things can help us explain what might otherwise feel like a complex move on the Navigator and support an expanded way of seeing and operating from the Third Way.

To help people explore and name the Third Way, get people to visualize bringing together the two poles. Describe the braiding of two strands of rope, the harmony of two combined notes, or putting together the nut and the bolt—whatever gives people a visual and practical way to see, and then articulate, their vision of the Third Way. It is often helpful to brainstorm a number of different options before settling on one that works best for the situation.

Let's use the example of Diplomacy::Candor with the nut and the bolt. Imagine you've helped a leadership team identify the benefits and overuses of each pole. They can now see the situation with a polarity mindset and understand their issue is not solvable and must be navigated over time to avoid the suffering occurring from their overuse of Diplomacy. They are also beginning to experience the magic that often happens when groups use a sensemaking tool to navigate paradoxical tension. People are beginning to listen to each other, the conversation is richer, and they have more courage to step into the vulnerability needed to look at their identity. As a result, a dialogue has begun that is allowing people to see the situation, each other, and themselves more completely.

At this point, you hold up the nut and ask the team to imagine it is Diplomacy. Then you hold up the bolt and ask them to imagine it is Candor. Now, you fasten the nut to the bolt, hold it in the air, and ask them to imagine them coming together as the Third Way. How would they name the two poles joined together in one state that contains both and eliminates neither? What would their experience be, and how would the organization experience *them*, if they showed up like this?

Of course, the possible names are endless and as unique as the individuals envisioning them. What's important is that the description works for the people navigating the polarity. It does not have to make sense to anyone else. It is about creating a type of mantra or metaphor that, when called upon, allows people to quickly step into the mindset of the Third Way and use it as a springboard for action. In this case, it might be similar to what Kim Scott[8] calls Radical Candor—the art of Challenging Directly and Caring Personally, or perhaps the group would call it Respectfully Honest, or Gentle Truth Sayer.

When helping individuals, teams, or organizations articulate the Third Way, questions like these can be useful:

- What would you *be* like to get the benefits of both poles in this situation?
- What would you be experiencing if you were holding both poles? What would you be feeling?
- How would other people experience you if you were getting the benefits of both poles?
- What is possible by harmonizing, or braiding, both poles?
- How would you see the world if you blended X and Y? What mindset would you hold?
- What would be true (about the situation and people in it) if you were holding both poles simultaneously? What mindset would you have?
- What image comes to mind when you think about how to describe this space—can you think of a metaphor?

Polarity	Possible Questions to Explore the Third Way	Possible Ways to Name the Third Way*
Candor::Diplomacy	What would you be like to get the benefits of both poles in this situation?	• Candidly connected • To the point *with* the person
	What mindset would we hold if we blended Candor and Diplomacy?	• Speak our minds with care • Hardball, soft bats

Polarity	Possible Questions to Explore the Third Way	Possible Ways to Name the Third Way*
Planned::Emergent	What image comes to mind when you think about how to describe this space—can you think of a metaphor?	• Finger paint by numbers • Clear plan, flexible path
	What is possible by harmonizing, or braiding, both poles?	• Efficient creativity • Off the beaten checklist
Directive Leadership:: Participative Leadership	How would other people experience us if we were getting the benefits of both poles?	• Inclusively decisive • Assured and affirming
	How would you see the world if you braided Directive and Participative Leadership together?	• With clear and curious eyes • Firm and open regard

Figure 3.6: Naming the Third Way

A key point here is that the Third Way doesn't have to make sense to anyone other than the person(s) creating the Navigator—it is their way of naming the harmonization to make sense and take action.

More Being, Less Doing

To navigate a polarity by standing in the transformational force of the Third Way, it is important that our effort—what we do—comes from a place of our being, who we are. Navigating Paradox as a human being is very different than trying to achieve it as a human *doing*. Doing is a strong diagonal in the United States and many other countries. Our preference for doing makes it tempting to jump straight to action in this part of the Navigator.

When working with the Third Way, you will likely hear people confuse the Third Way for strategies. When talking about the Third Way, they will describe what they can *do* to achieve it. The Third Way is more about who we *be*, how we show up, and how we feel in the space that harmonizes the two poles. Strategies, described in more detail below, are more about what we will DO to get more of the benefits, stay with the vulnerability, and monitor the polarity over time. To effectively Navigate Paradox, we need to navigate Do::Be, and the Transformational Third Way is a space to explicitly explore the being part of the dynamic.

One of the benefits of focusing on the Third Way as something we "be" as opposed to something we "do" is that it allows us to adopt a mindset that opens up an entire range of actions we likely hadn't noticed before. In the Candor::Diplomacy example above, using "Telling people what I think in meetings in a nice manner" as a Third Way provides one way to *do* it (which is better than nothing!). However, it doesn't open as many possible ways for action as does Respectfully Honest or Gentle Truth Sayer. Naming the Third Way in a form of *being* allows you to apply it in any type of situation by asking things like, "In this situation, how can I be the Gentle Truth Sayer?" or "What would it look like to be Respectfully Honest as I go into this conversation?" This allows us to brainstorm and explore a multitude of actions we can take to be in that space and to get the benefits of both poles. When we can *be* the Third Way, we can *do* much more of it, and that's where real transformation occurs.

Polarity	Example of a Third Way more like strategies (doing)	Example of Third Way focused on being— these are more helpful!
Candor::Diplomacy	Ask questions in meetings to help give voice to alternative opinions	Respectfully Honest -or- Gentle Truth Sayer
Planned::Emergent	Create a culture of listening and generating new ideas before making decisions	Structured Creativity -or- Vines on a Trellis
Directive::Participative	Identify decisions that will be handled solely by the leadership team and topics where input will be sought	Bringing Engaged Empowerment -or- Ask and Tell

Figure 3.7: Naming the Third Way—Moving From Doing To Being

If you hear more about *doing* when discussing the Third Way—more actions and strategies than *being*—you can take each of the actions and follow up with one or more of these questions to uncover the experience.

- If that were happening, what would you be experiencing? How would you be feeling?
- If you were doing that, how would you show up to the situation? How would others experience or describe you?
- How would you have to *be* in order to *do* that? What would be important? How, mentally, would you approach the situation?
- If you were doing that, what would you achieve—what state, or impact, would you be trying to make?
- What mindset would those actions spring from? You'd be thinking, "It's important that I…"

Case Example

"What would it be like to stand in a space where you were getting the benefits of both Compete and Collaborate? Let's brainstorm some options," Erica's coach suggested. Together, they began to create the list captured in Figure 3.8 on the following page. At one point, Erica said, "Well, I'd bring everyone on all the teams together to share ideas before we moved into fast action." Realizing this was more *doing* than *being*, the coach redirected her by asking, "That's a great strategy, but what would you *feel* like if you were doing that consistently—can you think of a metaphor?" Erica thought and then said, "It would be like I was the head lioness leading the pride out for a kill." After brainstorming a few other options, "Leading the Pride" was the Third Way Erica chose to step into.

Step Four—Vulnerability Throughway

The Vulnerability Throughway is the place on the Navigator that helps individuals, teams, and organizations name and explore what feels risky about holding both poles together. We have to be willing to travel through the Throughway to get to the Third Way, which is why on the Navigator the Third Way balances on the tip of Vulnerability. Like the Third Way, the Throughway isn't a knowing thing. It is an embodying thing. It, too, is a space of experience, being, and heart.

Stepping off our diagonal into the Third Way can be uncomfortable, even scary, and requires us to be OK with the inherent tension between the two poles. This is likely because, for many of us, our either/or mindset runs so deeply, it can seem impossible to embrace both poles of a polarity without threatening the values, benefits, or parts of our identity created by the pole we prefer.

POLARITY NAVIGATOR
Strategies

Compete

Benefits ⇧

We focus on excellence to win

People work fast

Individuals/I get big rewards

We hit stretch targets

Sr. Leadership is impressed because we exceed goals

Overuses ⇩

Teams try to destroy each other

We have blinders that limit ideas

Others are resentful/don't buy in

Teams get cut-throat and toxic

People don't share leads or info which limits business revenue

Collaborate

Benefits ⇧

I develop deeper relationships

We create synergy of ideas

Others buy in to our solutions

We trade leads to drive business

Sr. Leadership is happy because there is better morale

Overuses ⇩

We focus on feelings, not success

We involve everyone – it's slow

Rewards are shared, no incentive

Results and people are mediocre

We miss strategic goals

Transformational Third Way

Bigger Together

~~Bring everyone together to share leads, then move~~

Leading the Pride

Goals and group

For me and for them

Vulnerability Throughway

Figure 3.8: Compete::Collaborate Transformational Third Way

Being with this uncertainty, anxiety, and fear is at the heart of vulnerability and also the heart of standing in the Third Way. In fact, unless we are able to step into this space of vulnerability, we have little hope of actually maintaining the Third Way. Instead, we will retreat back to the comfort of our diagonal and the world as we know it.

The Vulnerability Throughway also allows us to explore and uncover assumptions we have about the world and how we operate in it. Kegan and Leahy[9] suggest that testing these types of assumptions can be intimidating enough to keep us from making the changes we say we want. Using the Navigator to uncover and be vulnerable to them allows us to experiment with the things that seem so risky and uncomfortable.

Usually, once we are standing fully in the Third Way and starting to experience the benefits of doing so, the things that felt risky begin to dissipate. The fears it seemed we were vulnerable to no longer feel so uncomfortable, and we are able to navigate the polarity with much more ease. The Throughway on the Navigator provides a safe space to explore and practice something most of us were taught to hide or avoid.

Tips for Exploring the Vulnerability Throughway

Choosing Courage over Comfort

Finding ways to help others understand our natural tendency to pull away from discomfort and name what feels risky about being with both "this" and "that" is important. Otherwise, they will not be able to stay with the Third Way and will retreat back to their diagonal. A metaphor that we often use is the finger trap toy you might have played with as a kid or even as an adult!

In case you didn't experience the joy (and anguish) of this toy as a kid, it is a simple puzzle that traps two of a person's fingers when inserted in the ends of a cylinder woven from bamboo. The initial, and natural, reaction is to pull your fingers outward to avoid the trap, but you learn quickly that pulling only tightens the trap. The only way to get free is to move your fingers toward the middle, which expands the openings and frees the fingers.

The experience of navigating a polarity can be quite similar. As we move to embrace more of our less-preferred pole, there are a number of triggers that can make us pull away rather than step in, which just tightens the trap.

- We might be scared that we will lose part of our identity (the benefits of our preferred pole).
- We could get frightened by the possibility we will become what we fear about our less-preferred pole (the overuses of that pole).
- We get uneasy about the unknown nature of the other pole.
- We anticipate the potential judgment we could face from those who hold the same preference as we do (as we step toward the other pole, we could threaten their values).

In any case, we might react to the discomfort by pulling away from, instead of stepping toward, the other pole. Like with the finger lock puzzle, the more we fight the discomfort, the more the contraction keeps us stuck in our way of seeing and closes off the possibilities found in the Third Way. Like the finger lock, to navigate the Third Way and embrace one pole without losing the benefits of the other, relax, get curious, and choose courage over comfort. When we do, we set ourselves free or, in this case, harmonize both poles.

Let's go back to the Diplomacy::Candor example explored above. Imagine the team describes the Third Way as Respectfully Honest and being known for developing deep trust by giving people greater clarity on where they stand. Now imagine you say, "If it were this simple, my guess is, you would already be getting the benefits of both. As we know, it oftentimes isn't this simple. What might feel risky about standing in the Third Way of Diplomacy::Candor for this team?"

At this point, it's likely you could experience a little bit of discomfort yourself — the discomfort of silence. It is important to remember that even sharing our thoughts about the Vulnerability Throughway can feel vulnerable. In those instances, simply naming the vulnerability is in and of itself an act of courage. After a few minutes of silence, you bring back out the finger lock, place your fingers in either side and pull, asking, "What might cause you to pull away from the benefits of Candor and retreat back to the safety of Diplomacy?" And out it comes — "losing talent," "alienating our donors," "the possibility of hurting someone or bruising relationships," "being seen as cold and heartless," "being seen as challenging authority." The only way for the team to step into the Third Way is to name these fears and test their assumptions.

When helping individuals, teams, or organizations articulate the Vulnerability Throughway, questions like these can be useful:

- What feels risky about holding both poles together?
- What would be the most uncomfortable part of standing in the Third Way?
- What do you have to be OK with in order to braid together both poles?
- What part of who you are, or what you value, needs to shift or expand to stand in the Third Way?
- What is at stake for you if you step into the Third Way?
- What would you need to "loosen up on" in order to blend both poles?
- What needs to be held, or remembered, to integrate the poles?

Polarity	Possible Questions to Explore the Vulnerability Throughway	Possible Ways to Name the Vulnerability Throughway*
Candor::Diplomacy	What feels risky about holding the poles together?	People will see me as fake and just a "yes man"
	What do we have to be OK with in order to braid together both poles?	The fact that some people aren't going to like what we have to say
Planned::Emergent	What is at stake for you if you step into the Third Way?	Missing the deadline
	What needs to be held, or remembered, as we integrate the poles?	It's OK for us to not have all the answers as we start the process
Directive Leadership:: Participative Leadership	What would be the most uncomfortable part of standing in the Third Way?	I'd have to give up control and be OK not having people do it my way
	What would we need to "loosen up on" in order to blend both poles?	Some people will be upset when they don't get a vote in the decision

Figure 3.9: Naming the Vulnerability Throughway

* A key point here is that the Vulnerability will be different for everyone—and what feels really risky for one person may not seem risky at all for another.

Different Types and Depth of Vulnerability

When working with a group, it is likely you will have some people who prefer one diagonal and some who prefer the other.

In these cases, the vulnerability will look very different, so be sure to create space for all points of view. Likewise, even individuals who hold the same diagonal will vary in their responses to the risks of stepping into the Third Way. Agreement, here, is not the point, so capture them all. The point is to build awareness about what the group, and individuals in the group, need to be open to in order to begin navigating the polarity more effectively.

The responses to the questions about vulnerability typically vary in how "deep" they are. One person might name a vulnerability as "I'd miss my sales targets," while another person referring to the same polarity says, "I would lose my capacity to love." In these situations, it's important to meet the person or team where they are rather than insert your own ideas of what might feel risky to you. While not always necessary, if you want to push yourself, or others, to examine the risk a bit more deeply, after answering the questions above, follow up with questions such as these:

- What would be so bad about that?
- What's the biggest thing that would be at risk if that happened?
- What about that feels scary or uncomfortable?

These questions can also be helpful if the vulnerability named is similar to one of the overuses of the pole being moved toward. Remember, the reason we don't embrace the other pole is often because we fear, or don't want, its overuses. Therefore, one or more of the items in the overuses can get called out in the Vulnerability Throughway. There's nothing wrong with this, and you can explore it more and go deeper by asking questions like the three above.

After exploring the Throughway and naming the vulnerability, it can be useful to spend time considering which of the risks are real risks and which might be assumptions. Often, the items identified in this part of the Navigator are things we *assume* will happen by stepping into the Third Way. Testing these assumptions is key to identifying sustained actions for navigating the polarity.

Case Example

"As you think about loosening up on Compete and stepping toward Collaborate into the Third Way, what feels risky?" asked the coach. Without hesitation, Erica blurted out, "That's easy. I'd miss my targets!" Nodding her head and pointing to the bottom right quadrant, the coach said, "That's definitely a potential over-use of Collaborate and we've captured it in this quadrant...I'm curious, what would be so bad about missing your goals? What about that would be most uncomfortable?" As they explored the space, they discovered Erica had a concern that if she stopped being so competitive, she'd be "seen as soft and not a go-getter" and would likely miss the promotion she was hoping for. This was a real fear that would likely keep her from embracing the Third Way. After some coaching and exploration, she realized it was an assumption that she'd have to explore because the advancement she craved actually required her to be more collaborative without losing her competitive edge. See Figure 3.10 on following page.

Step Five—Strategies

The strategies section of the Navigator captures the actions that allow you to do any number of things: stand in the Third Way, get the benefits from each pole, step into the vulnerability, and monitor the polarity over time. It is the action plan for how you will successfully navigate the polarity. This piece of the process is crucial—the whole reason of making sense is to take action in the world. Standing in the Third Way can be difficult, so we need specific strategies for doing *and* being in order to do so.

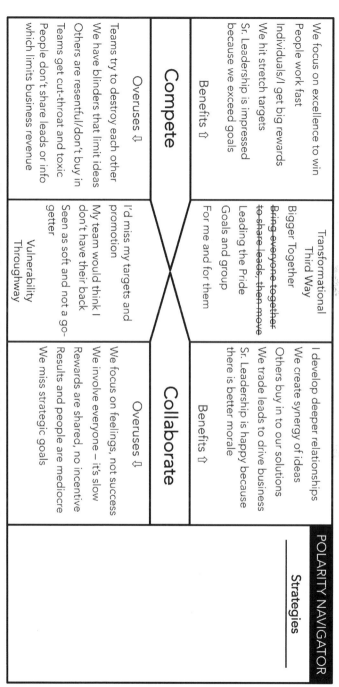

Compete		**Collaborate**
Benefits ⇧	**Transformational Third Way**	**Benefits ⇧**
We focus on excellence to win People work fast Individuals/I get big rewards We hit stretch targets Sr. Leadership is impressed because we exceed goals	Bigger Together ~~Bring everyone together to share leads, then move~~ Leading the Pride Goals and group For me and for them	I develop deeper relationships We create synergy of ideas Others buy in to our solutions We trade leads to drive business Sr. Leadership is happy because there is better morale
Overuses ⇩	**Vulnerability Throughway**	**Overuses ⇩**
Teams try to destroy each other We have blinders that limit ideas Others are resentful/don't buy in Teams get cut-throat and toxic People don't share leads or info which limits business revenue	I'd miss my targets and promotion My team would think I don't have their back Seen as soft and not a go-getter	We focus on feelings, not success We involve everyone – it's slow Rewards are shared, no incentive Results and people are mediocre We miss strategic goals

POLARITY NAVIGATOR

Strategies

Figure 3.10: Compete::Collaborate Vulnerability Throughway

Strategies for navigating a polarity typically require us to think creatively and do some brainstorming. Questions such as these can be helpful for identifying strategies:

- What actions will you take to stand in the Third Way?
- How could you get more of the benefits of Y *without losing* the benefits of X?
- In this situation, what actions could you take to demonstrate you're (*insert the Third Way*)?
- Is there a specific benefit you need to achieve? What actions would let you achieve it without going too far?
- What can you do to step into, and stay with, the vulnerability that arises when pursuing the Third Way?
- How can the tension of the polarity creatively occupy your heart?
- Movement requires courage and comfort. What courageous action is needed to stand in the Third Way—what would courage do?
- What will you do to monitor this polarity over time?

Tips for Creating Strategies

Have a Good Process

There are several key steps to identifying solid strategies, which are not unlike other action-planning processes.

1. **Brainstorm.** Creating good actions is sometimes best done "off the map." Brainstorm on another piece of paper so as not to make the process feel final by writing everything on the Navigator.
2. **Prioritize.** Evaluate the list to identify the most beneficial and realistic actions. As with any planning process, balance the level of impact, effort, and feasibility of actions.

3. **Check.** Agree upon the strategies and then ask, "If we were doing all of these things, would we be experiencing the Third Way?" If not, what else would need to be done?

4. **Specify.** If working in a group, make sure action items are written in a way that outlines who will do what by when, as you would with any well-written plans.

5. **Ensure.** Agree on an accountability structure to ensure follow-through on actions and to continue to effectively navigate the polarity.

Small Experiments

Polarities are complex. A common tip to dealing with complexity is to try small actions, see how they go, and adjust as needed. This can also be true when creating strategies. If it's not completely clear what you would have to do to stand squarely in the Third Way, take a step back. What are some small things you might do that would help move you in that direction? What experiments might you run? What could you do to reach out and touch the other pole? For example, someone looking to loosen up on the Participative Leadership pole in order to embrace more of the Directive Leadership pole might choose a small experiment like, *"At the beginning of the week, I'll tell my team that I'm open to their input but that the point isn't consensus in this case, and I will make the decision by Friday. We'll see how that goes!"* It's important in these cases to identify how you will monitor the results of your experiment and how you will know when it is time to move on to your next experiment.

Balancing Benefits

Sometimes, actions will be identified that correspond to the specific benefits of one of the poles. This is fine, but a word of warning. It's important that both poles have actions that will help the system reap the benefits of the polarity, so make sure the actions balance out in a way that moves you toward the Third Way. If you have several actions to achieve the benefits of one pole and none for the other, there's a good chance you might head toward the overuses of that pole.

Start-Stop-Continue-Modify

Strategies can fall into at least four categories. The first contains things that can be started. These are new actions that would help the individual or system stand in the Third Way or get the benefits of one of the poles. The second type of actions are behaviors or activities that can be stopped. These "stop" actions typically, but don't always, pertain to eliminating things that are producing the overuse of a pole as a way to alleviate some of the current pain and downsides.

It is also important to include actions that the system will "continue" in order to keep getting the benefits it is currently getting. If the system is experiencing the overuses of a pole, it is highly probable they are already doing things to experience the benefits of that pole but just taking them too far. In these cases, it's important that the system not throw the baby out with the bathwater and so should likely continue some of the things they are currently doing to maintain the benefits of the pole they don't want to lose. Likewise, they may choose to "modify" something they are already doing so that it more accurately reflects the Third Way. Being explicit about the things that will continue will also help lower some of the resistance that might be evoked when announcing the newly identified actions.

Case Example

As she thought about what it would look like to "Lead the Pride," Erica was able to develop strategies that would help her stand in the Third Way and achieve many of the benefits from both poles. One was the item she originally identified when discussing the Third Way—bringing the teams together to share leads. During the process, her coach also asked her, "Is there anything you should continue doing, or modify slightly?" Erica was quick to note that she should continue to set stretch targets for her team, but that she'd do it a little differently and try to bring Antonio into the process so that it wasn't such a competition. The coach also asked, "What can you watch for that would let you know you are getting too much Compete?" Erica's response was to listen to her team—if they "start trash-talking Antonio's team, then I'd know things are getting a bit too competitive." Erica's coach sensed her next question might be a tough and important one for Erica to consider. Her coach asked, "What can you do to step into, and stay with, your concern of being seen as soft and not as a go-getter as you pursue the Third Way?" Erica decided that when she noticed this assumption surfacing, she would pause and ask herself, "Is this really true?" She also realized she needed some help just noticing when the assumption surfaces. Before they finished, they identified a way that Erica would monitor the polarity over time—how she would keep an eye on it, knowing that it could not be solved, only navigated. See Figure 3.11 on following page.

POLARITY NAVIGATOR

Strategies

1. Bring teams together to share leads and ideas two times a year
2. Establish cross-team *Competitive Intel Group*
3. Meet monthly with Antonio to share strategies and challenges
4. Explore possibility of two shared targets across teams
5. Listen for increased trash-talking of Antonio's team by my team
6. Continue to set stretch goals and help Antonio see how/why he should do the same
7. Be mindful of the "soft-not-a-go-getter" assumption and ask "Is this true?" when it shows up
8. To monitor: Make this a regular agenda item in my one-on-ones with Antonio and supervisor

---

Transformational Third Way

Bigger Together

~~Bring everyone together to share leads, then move~~

Leading the Pride

Goals and group

For me and for them

Compete — Benefits ⇧

- We focus on excellence to win
- People work fast
- Individuals/I get big rewards
- We hit stretch targets
- Sr. Leadership is impressed because we exceed goals

Collaborate — Benefits ⇧

- I develop deeper relationships
- We create synergy of ideas
- Others buy in to our solutions
- We trade leads to drive business
- Sr. Leadership is happy because there is better morale

Compete — Overuses ⇩

- Teams try to destroy each other
- We have blinders that limit ideas
- Others are resentful/don't buy in
- Teams get cut-throat and toxic
- People don't share leads or info which limits business revenue

Collaborate — Overuses ⇩

- We focus on feelings, not success
- We involve everyone – it's slow
- Rewards are shared, no incentive
- Results and people are mediocre
- We miss strategic goals

I'd miss my targets and promotion

My team would think I don't have their back

Seen as soft and not a go-getter

Vulnerability Throughway

Figure 3.11: Compete::Collaborate Strategies

Conclusion

Mapping a polarity can be both simple and complex. The steps outlined here provide a formulaic process for walking through and completing a Navigator that can help individuals, groups, and organizations make sense of, and take action to more effectively navigate any polarity. While the process outlined here may seem prescriptive, as if there is only one right way, don't let that stop you from taking action. Experience shows that most groups do not complete the steps in this order and, sometimes, may not complete the entire process. It's more important to do *something* than to do nothing for fear of not doing it 100% accurately. Most importantly, the process of mapping helps groups strengthen (or find!) their both/and thinking and vulnerability muscles, which are invaluable to driving different conversations in a world that far too often Suffers Paradox.

In Summary:

There are five key areas to complete when using the Polarity Navigator:

1. Pole Names — Create neutral names for each of the poles.

2. Benefits and Overuses — Identify the good things each pole brings and the problems that arise when there's too much of it.

3. The Transformational Third Way — Discover how you would be, not do, when the poles were braided or harmonized.

4. The Vulnerability Throughway — Explore the risks and courage needed to step into the Third Way.

5. Strategies — Create actions to navigate the polarity from the Third Way and monitor it over time.

POLARITY NAVIGATOR

Strategies

- What actions will you take to achieve the things outlined in the Third Way?
- How could you get more of the benefits of Y without losing the benefits of X?
- What can you do to stay with the vulnerability that arises when pursuing the Third Way?
- How can the tension creatively occupy your heart?
- Movement requires Courage and Comfort. What courageous action is needed to stand in the Third Way – what would Courage do?
- What can you do to experience and act from a place of integration?
- What will you do to Monitor this polarity over time?

Transformational Third Way

- What would it look like/feel like to have the benefits of both poles in this situation?
- What is possible by, or the impact of, harmonizing both poles?
- How do you see the world if you blended X and Y?
- What mindset would result from holding both poles simultaneously?
- What would you be experiencing if you were holding both poles?
- How would other people be experiencing you if you were holding both?

Benefits ⇑

- What benefits occur as a result of focusing on/showing up with this pole?
- What positive impacts does this pole bring to the situation?
- How does this pole contribute to overall success?

Benefits ⇑

Pole Y

Overuses ⇓

- When this pole is overused – when there is too much of it – what happens?
- What occurs when this pole is taken too far?
- What happens when this pole is focused on to the neglect/exclusion of the other pole?

Benefits ⇑

- What benefits occur as a result of focusing on/showing up with this pole?
- What positive impacts does this pole bring to the situation?
- How does this pole contribute to overall success?

Benefits ⇑

Pole X

Overuses ⇓

- When this pole is overused – when there is too much of it – what happens?
- What occurs when this pole is taken too far?
- What happens when this pole is focused on to the neglect/exclusion of the other pole?

Vulnerability Throughway

- What feels risky about holding both poles together?
- What would you need to "loosen up on" in order to blend both poles?
- What needs to be held, or remembered, to integrate the poles?
- What would be the most uncomfortable part of standing in the Third Way?
- What do you have to be OK with in order to blend both poles?
- What part of who you are, or what you value, needs to shift/expand?
- What's at stake for you if you step into the Third Way?

Figure 3.12: The Navigator Tool

CHAPTER 4

THE PROCESS OF NAVIGATING POLARITIES

We've examined what polarities are, how they work, and how to create maps to navigate them. But what process do people use to actually work with polarities? How do they apply this information, mindset, and toolset to make a difference in their lives and organizations? This chapter outlines a typical process used by leaders, coaches, and practitioners to work with polarities and then explores several cases as practical examples. These cases, while informative, will not be exhaustive. The follow-up books in this series provide much more detail into how polarities are navigated in different sectors and situations.

The Process of Navigating Polarities

It's not surprising that there is no single correct method of using polarities to create a both/and mindset. Since Barry Johnson's book *Polarity Management*,[1] individuals and organizations around the world have been using various forms of his sense-making map to help navigate paradoxical tensions. As a result, there are numerous methodologies and processes, depending on the user. In fact, as you read follow-up books in this series, you will encounter multiple approaches and methods.

For the most part, the process outlined below is similar to the approaches followed by other expert users of polarities, but there are several differences based on the use of the Polarity Navigator. To be effective, one must first analyze whether the situation contains a polarity to be navigated or a problem to be solved. If it's a polarity, the next step is to map the interdependent pair in order to make sense of it and ensure that "you have it, it doesn't have you." You must then connect to the polarity by identifying the Third Way and the vulnerability needed to experience it. Then, you must act by creating and advancing the strategies identified to navigate the paradox. Finally, because a polarity is never-ending and cannot be solved, you must monitor your progress and revisit any previous steps as needed. Again, different practitioners and organizations call these steps by different names and often include additional steps based on their specific needs and focus, but most successful efforts will follow some form of these basic steps.

Navigating Polarities in Five Steps

ANALYZE to See	MAP to Understand	EXPLORE to Connect	ACT to Expand	MONITOR to Discern
Problem or Polarity?	Benefits and Overuses	Third Way and Vulnerability	Strategies and Actions	Watch and Adjust

Figure 4.1

Analyze to See

The first step in navigating a polarity is to look at a situation and determine, or see, whether the issue is a problem or a polarity. This is perhaps the most important *and* most difficult of the five steps. So much so that Chapter 5 is dedicated solely to how to recognize polarities and provides specific tips and tricks for knowing when, and when not, to use a polarity lens.

When analyzing an issue or situation to see if there is a polarity at play, there are two initial criteria to consider. Each is outlined below with a rationale and example. Again, Chapter 5 goes much more deeply into this topic and provides many other ways of seeing, but if either of the following is true, you are likely dealing with a polarity.

**Over time, the situation requires the benefits of both "sides,"
or arguments, for success.** Both poles of a polarity have benefits
unique to that pole, and both sets of those benefits are needed
for the system to be successful over time. The key here is "over
time." Candor and Diplomacy both have unique benefits, and,
over time, a leader needs the benefits of both to be successful. The
same isn't necessarily true with two alternatives of a problem. If
the issue you're dealing with needs the benefits of both options,
a polarity lens will likely be useful.

**The situation is the result of overusing a strength or having
"too much of a good thing."** In a polarity, issues occur when we
overuse one of the poles. If the issue you're dealing with is the
result of taking something too far, or over-focusing on a value
or approach, a polarity lens will likely be useful. For example,
if teachers feel neglected in a school system that prides itself on
"putting students first," there is a likelihood the overuse of the
value is creating a problem, so using polarities as an approach
would be beneficial.

When faced with an issue or opportunity, running it through
these two lenses can provide insight into whether or not there is
a polarity at play. We'll dig deeper in the next chapter, but for
now, why should anyone care about figuring out the difference
between a problem and a polarity?

The world is becoming increasingly complex. The interconnectedness of the global community, the speed at which we share
information, and the uncertainty facing humans all work together
to create incredibly complex problems. *Problems.* While many
of these situations involve polarities that need to be navigated,
many are simply (or complexly!) problems that require either/
or thinking. For example, how do we address the college-loan
debt crises? Treating problems like polarities can be a waste of
time and resources and will likely lead to more frustration and
increased complexity.

That said, there are an abundance of issues that clearly contain polarities. If we treat these polarity situations as if they were problems by using an either/or mindset, the system will Suffer Paradox. This means that not only will we *not* effectively deal with the presenting issue, but there will also be negative impacts on morale, communication, relationships, and the ability to effectively and quickly deal with future problematic issues. Seeing these issues for what they are and using a polarity lens can help drive different conversations and produce more sustainable and transformational solutions.

It's important to note here that there are many problems that have one or more polarities contained within, or beneath, them. For example, a decision of whether or not we should drill for oil in a national park seems like a problem—while there are benefits to each position, we don't necessarily need both sets of benefits over time. Likewise, it doesn't seem like the problem is a result of us overusing a value. However, if we look underneath the problem, there are several polarities at play, one of which is Protect Our Resources::Use Our Resources. Chapter 5 pulls apart these types of issues to clarify additional ways to see.

Stepping back to analyze whether an issue is a problem or a polarity is a critical step in the process. Knowing how to do so effectively is an important skill that can save lots of headaches and missteps. Without it, we are unable to pay attention to any of the following steps, especially, mapping.

Map to Understand

Once you've determined the issue or opportunity does, in fact, deal with a polarity, you need a way to make sense of the impacts it's having. The best way to do this is to create a map of how the polarity dynamic is at work in the situation. The process outlined in Chapter 3 provides everything needed in order to generate a useful map using the Polarity Navigator. Begin by including stakeholders to the greatest degree possible, then name the polarity. Through conversation and dialogue, identify the benefits and overuses of each pole to help people make the polarity object so that they have it and it doesn't have them.

An important element of "Map to Understand" lies in the word "understand." Completing a map by filling in the components is important, but an ultimate goal of this step is the dialogue and "meaning making" that comes by creating the map. Our research shows that it is in the process of completing a map that groups begin to Navigate Paradox. The dialogue leads to increased understanding and helps individuals see that both poles, and thereby both points of view, are necessary for success in the long term. Therefore, don't shortchange this step by having one person complete a map for an entire organization. Understanding happens as a result of creating the map, not necessarily due to the map itself.

Explore to Connect

One of the unique and powerful aspects of using the Polarity Navigator is the ability to provide people with a way to connect to the polarity dynamic at a deeper and richer level of understanding. The Transformational Third Way creates the space to reintegrate the poles after they have been differentiated in the Map to Understand step, above. This place of reintegration allows people to create a vision of what *the experience* would be like having both poles exist simultaneously. Without this step it is easy to revert to a contingency strategy (picking whatever pole seems most needed) or a separation strategy (focusing on each pole at different times or by different parts of the system) when working with the polarity dynamic.

Connecting deeply to a vision of standing in the Third Way is important because, as discussed in Chapter 3, the Third Way often requires us to explore the vulnerability we might experience as we loosen up on a pole that has felt comfortable and served us well. Denying this and pretending that navigating to the Third Way will be easy is a setup for more frustration. The Vulnerability Throughway allows individuals to identify and be with what feels risky or uncomfortable about stepping toward the needed pole without losing the benefits of the pole they love.

Helping people connect to the vision of the harmonized poles and having them embrace the vulnerability it will take to do so allows them to experience the dynamic of the polarity more deeply. This increases their understanding and the way they make sense of the situation, thus allowing them to navigate the polarity more effectively. It also allows for more robust and sustainable strategies created in the next step of the process.

Act to Expand

Navigating polarities requires intentional action over time, so creating and acting on strategies is an integral piece of the process. As highlighted in Chapter 3, two of the things that strategies can be based on are what it will take to stand in the Third Way and what is needed to step into the Vulnerability Throughway. Creating these plans allows people to act to expand not only the way they navigate this polarity but also their impact and effectiveness in the world.

However, as with any change or initiative, the plan is only as good as the degree to which you actually implement it. The same is true for the Navigator. The purpose of helping someone make sense of a polarity is so it can serve as a platform for action. Without the latter, there is little hope that an individual or system will navigate the polarity well. Ensuring that the strategies created during the mapping are realistic and defined in a way that drives accountability is an important first step in this process.

Depending on the size of the initiative, strategies may need their own project tracker. Actions can be put on agendas or schedules for check-ins to ensure accountability. Use whatever platform or methodology your team or organization uses to track progress and drive action. Unfortunately, we have seen groups have rich conversations and create beautiful Navigators, and then fall short when it comes to implementing the plan. They don't act and, therefore, never effectively navigate or harness the creative tension that allows them to expand more fully into the power of the polarity.

Monitor to Discern

No matter how brilliant the strategies, you will never solve the polarity. As frustrating as it may sound to some, you will never be able to cross the polarity off your list of to-dos—the system will never be "done" with it. You can only manage the polarity and work to experience the Third Way by paying attention to, and integrating, both poles over time. This requires the system to monitor the polarity—to keep an eye on the energy to ensure that one pole isn't being inadvertently privileged, thus risking the possibility of reaping its overuses.

To be sure the system effectively monitors the dynamic, it is helpful to identify specific actions to do so as part of your strategies. These plans should aim to help the individual or system discern how they are navigating the polarity and what they might need to do on the next step in the journey. There are numerous ways to monitor the polarity over time, but given that one of the main aims of using the Navigator is to help people drive different conversations, the most effective is through dialogue.

The simplest way to monitor a polarity is through discussion with key players and stakeholders. Once created, the Navigator can be a powerful conversation tool. It is an awareness and action tracker that contains the wisdom of multiple perspectives, each important to the long-term success of the system. We have worked with groups who do an exceptional job of monitoring a polarity simply by revisiting the Navigator and discussing how they are doing against it. In such cases, have everyone look at the map and consider questions like these:

- Overall, how well are we navigating this polarity?
- In what ways are we experiencing the Third Way, or not?
- What are we learning?
- Which of the benefits are we getting? Are there benefits we need more of?
- Are we paying attention to one pole more than the other? Is that sustainable?
- Are we experiencing (or anticipating that we'll experience) any of the overuses?
- Have we been staying with the vulnerability needed to experience the Third Way?
- When are we choosing courage over comfort? When are we choosing comfort over courage?

The answers to these questions can lead to creating new strategies or revisiting others that may not have been fully executed as planned.

The important part of this process is the discussion that occurs—listening and seeking to understand are crucial parts of monitoring the dynamic of a polarity. When people Suffer Paradox, they stop listening, or perhaps, when people stop listening, they Suffer Paradox. Discerning requires the curiosity and courage to question and a capacity to be honest with ourselves and each other. The point is to use the Navigator as an ongoing way to value all perspectives and commit to a dialogue that allows you to discern how you are doing and to determine the next steps in navigating the polarity.

Monitoring allows the system to continue holding the polarity as object so that we have it instead of it having us. The polarity will never be solvable, but by continuing to monitor it, we can be sure we don't revert back to our preferred and comfortable diagonal. It often takes time and practice to stand in the Third Way, but the good news is the polarity isn't going away, so we'll have lots of opportunity to practice. It is often the simple act of practicing and experimenting that allows us to harness the creative tension of a polarity in a way that leads our teams and organizations to higher levels of effectiveness. What follows are several examples of individuals and teams that have done just that.

Cases to Explore

The following cases and corresponding Navigators demonstrate various aspects of the five-step process as well as a variety of points highlighted earlier in the book. The topics include:

- **A Hospital — Seeing Others' Benefits:** Members of a team get unstuck and drastically improve results because they could see each other more completely.

- **A Coaching 360 — Using the Diagonals:** A coach uses a polarity lens to help a client make sense of 360° feedback to drive awareness, acceptance, and action.

- **Organizational Structure — Stopping the Pendulum Swing and Engaging Stakeholders:** A company prevents a swing of the pendulum during a restructuring, creatively involves stakeholders, and finds wisdom in the resistance.

- **Framing a Change Effort — Expand without Losing:** An organization realizes navigating a polarity is not about giving up what made them great.

A Hospital—Seeing Others' Benefits

Background

The CEO of a hospital system was having trouble with his senior team. Morale was low, communication was strained, relationships were damaged, and the team wasn't making significant progress against any of the goals they'd set for themselves or the three hospitals in the system. After interviewing the team members, it became apparent that there were (at least) two camps in the group, one that rallied behind the Chief Financial Officer (CFO) and the other behind the Chief Nursing Officer (CNO).

When describing the CFO, the CNO said, "She is so controlling and focused on money that she doesn't care about the impact on quality of care or patient-satisfaction scores," and "She puts tons of extra stress on our already overworked employees because she doesn't care about their well-being." The CFO, on the other hand, talked about the CNO saying things like, "He has no clue what it takes to keep the lights on or to keep people paid," and "He doesn't care that his fiscal irresponsibility impacts our long-term ability to serve the community."

Because the team seemed to be experiencing the symptoms of Suffering Paradox, and the two key players were describing each other in terms that could be the overuses of a pole, it seemed a polarity lens would be useful in this situation. In actuality, the tension experienced by this team is quite common in many organizations: focusing on mission and focusing on fiscal health. At a hospital, this could be called Focus on Patient Health::Focus on Fiscal Health, Mission::Margin, Run a Hospital::Run a Business, or many others. Ultimately, the team decided to name their polarity Business Focus::Patient Focus.

The Process

The team came together and, as part of the intervention, learned about polarities and how the dynamic works in systems. The team then created a Navigator of Business Focus::Patient Focus by using flip charts around the room (as described later in this chapter). When all of the benefits and overuses were identified, the flip charts were hung together on the wall on either side of the Third Way and the Throughway. A simplified version of the Navigator is presented in Figure 4.2 [page 102].

As part of processing the map, the team was asked to look at each of the diagonals and to identify which point of view they naturally held. In that moment, the CFO said, "Oh, my God. I get it." She looked across the room to the CNO and said, "You're not wrong...and I'm not wrong...we're caught in this dynamic and both of us are right...we need this to coexist without it killing us." When dealing with a polarity, both points of view are accurate, but neither is complete. The process helped both parties see that they needed each other for sustained success and how the tension in the polarity had morphed into tension in the team. Creating a Navigator allowed the group to make the polarity object and "have it."

To be clear, things were not a picnic after that — there was still much work to be done. Mapping the polarity didn't make things better immediately, but it allowed for different conversations and provided the doorway for a different approach to action. The Vulnerability Throughway allowed them to identify what felt risky for them as a group, and as individuals, as they thought about the work it would take to lead from the Third Way. In addition to the strategies the group agreed upon, the CNO and CFO (as well as their respective "camps") came up with this challenge: *Whenever you start to get frustrated with someone, stop and consider the benefits their diagonal brings to the hospital and our patients — they want the benefits, not the overuses.*

POLARITY NAVIGATOR

Strategies

1. Re-engineer KPIs: $+Quality + Service
2. Review policies to eliminate rigid controls
3. Review financial authority levels, e.g., Purchasing /HR
4. Review resource availability for initiatives
5. Assistance in developing balanced scorecard for all metrics for SNS
6. Enhance employee education on all aspects of patient satisfaction
7. Sr. Administrators start rounding
8. Skill development and training
9. To monitor: Track actions – next steps at year end

Business Focus

Benefits ⇧

1. Growth of services and therapies
2. Employees paid well/competitive
3. Financial success
4. Expansion of facilities
5. Easy & thorough processes
6. Appropriate controls - accountability

Patient Focus

Benefits ⇧

1. Better care and outcomes
2. High employee satisfaction
3. Exceed mission of care & healing
4. Great quality! Great reputation
5. Sharing control and authority
6. Meets requirements for resources

Transformational Third Way

Fiscal health for patient health

Other Options:
1. Fiscally-minded care providers
2. Care is everyone's bottom line
3. Everyone is connected to care and finances

Business Focus — Overuses ⇩

1. Low-quality patient care
2. Poor employee satisfaction
3. Fail mission of care & healing
4. No patients b/c bad reputation
5. Excessive controls – slow care
6. Inadequate resources – save money

Patient Focus — Overuses ⇩

1. Eliminate services and therapies
2. Wage freeze and layoffs
3. Poor financial performance
4. Outdated facilities
5. Chaos & mayhem – no processes
6. No accountability controls

Vulnerability Throughway

1. Some waste while we empower and educate
2. Spend time focusing on areas we aren't naturally drawn to
3. Focusing on areas without clear and obvious rewards
4. CFO – Be OK if rankings slip this year
5. CMO – being perceived as a sell-out

Figure 4.2: Business Focus::Patient Focus

Takeaways

Seeing "the other" in terms of the overuses of the pole they hold while neglecting to see the benefits they bring creates a limiting and harmful perspective of our teams, organizations, and society. It's a clue a polarity is at play (discussed more in the next chapter) and that using a map as a way for people to make sense of the tension would be useful. In these cases, helping people relate to one another differently by simply discussing the benefits and overuses can be the most powerful part of the process. It gets them unstuck, which allows the energy to flow toward more effective strategies.

Another takeaway from this case is that this polarity shows up in different forms in almost every organization. Practice Law::Run a Firm, Serve the Homeless::Pay our Staff, Get Medicines to Patients::Have Money for R&D. The tension exists everywhere. Without a way to make sense of it, people often take sides and see one vantage point getting in the way of the other. The tension then "has them" and the organization will begin to Suffer Paradox. Helping people make sense through a polarity lens can make the opposite happen, harnessing the tension for creative synergy and better overall effectiveness.

A Coaching 360—Using the Diagonals

Background

As part of a coaching engagement with a Sr. Executive, a 360-degree feedback process was used to help ascertain potential development areas for the client. People were interviewed to discuss the client's strengths and areas of potential improvement. As a result of the interviews, it became clear that, among other things, the overuses from over-focusing on several poles were impacting his overall effectiveness.

The people who were interviewed said things like,

- "He destroys relationships because he has no regard for other people's feelings."
- "Well, he definitely lets you know where he stands—he doesn't beat around the bush."
- "People hesitate to share ideas or bring him into conversations because he can be brutal—it doesn't feel collaborative."
- "He ticks people off, so they write him off and work around him."

All of these suggest that he has a preference for, and was probably over-focusing on, Candor.

Since this client knew a bit about polarities, it made sense to use the framework as a potential lens to help him make sense of Candor::Diplomacy and to examine the resistance he might have to shifting a bit more toward the Diplomacy pole. The client agreed, and in one of his sessions, he and the coach created a Navigator to use as an ongoing resource and reference point.

The Process

Mapping in this case started off beautifully. When asked to come up with benefits of Candor, the client listed them in a rapid-fire sequence. He could hardly write fast enough to keep up with his ideas. *"Candor makes things happen faster. You don't have to tiptoe and beat around the bush. People know exactly where you stand, there's no guessing."* He quickly listed these and the other items in the benefits of Candor quadrant in the map in Figure 4.3 [page 106] (a simplified version of his map).

That's when things got tricky. When asked to list some of the overuses of Candor he said, in all seriousness, *"There aren't really any ways to overuse Candor. It's important that people know where you stand, that you don't beat around the bush...*" He basically began to reiterate all of the benefits he had just listed. True story.

Instead of pushing the issue, they decided to move along to the benefits of Diplomacy. When asked what the upsides of Diplomacy were, the client was very slow to come up with possibilities. It was a *very* slow struggle, and the coach ended up having to help in the brainstorming. Little by little they were able to populate the quadrant with things like *"There are strong relationships from listening," "People seek out feedback on new ideas,"* and the other things in Figure 4.3 [page 106].

As with the benefits of Candor, the overuses of Diplomacy came almost too quickly to capture. *"People can't trust that you're telling the truth," "It takes forever to get to the point," "You're seen as a doormat because you won't stand up for what you believe in."* At this point, it was really easy to point out how lopsided the map was, which begged the question: what might be missing?

Utilizing the rule that the diagonals on a Polarity Navigator are opposites, the coach said, "With a polarity, the diagonal quadrants are opposites, just as you've listed them here in the benefits of Candor and the overuses of Diplomacy. If that's the case, then the same must be true on the other diagonal—the overuses of Candor must be the opposite of the benefits of Diplomacy. For kicks, let's take everything we've written in the upsides of Diplomacy and write the exact opposite of that in the downside of Candor."

As the client started to transfer the opposites, he stopped midway through, saying, *"Crap. These are all the things people said about me in the 360."* It was a sobering moment, but the map provided a great way for him to make sense of the data and to see that the downsides he was getting were the result of overusing a strength that had made him really good. Up to a point.

With this new awareness, they moved into the Third Way. When asked, "How would people experience you if you brought the benefits of both Candor *and* Diplomacy to your leadership?" the client struggled to come off of his diagonal because quite a bit of his identity had been wrapped up in the benefits of Candor. The coach reminded him that developing as a leader wasn't about *giving up* the things he valued or gave him his edge. Instead, it was about loosening up on the pole he preferred and finding ways to bring a bit more Diplomacy into his style *without losing* the upsides of Candor.

With that, the client relaxed a bit and after a few awkward moments of silence said, "Candidly Caring. People would experience me as Candidly Caring if I brought both Candor and Diplomacy to my leadership." Appreciating that the Third Way is a place of courage and with courage comes risk, the coach moved to the Vulnerability Throughway and asked, "What feels risky to you about loosening up on Candor?" Without hesitation the client said, "I never want to be seen as weak," which led to an even richer conversation as they moved to strategies.

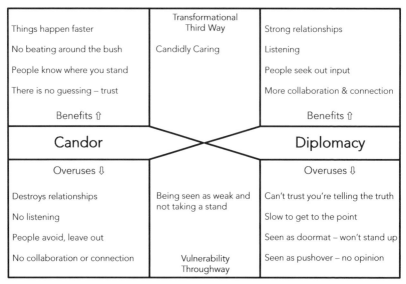

Figure 4.3: Candor::Diplomacy

Takeaways

This case highlights a number of key points. The first is observing the energy people have when filling out different quadrants on a map. Typically, when filling out a map, people will have more energy, and content will flow much more easily, for the benefits of the pole they prefer *and* the overuses of their less-preferred pole. It makes their diagonal really clear and can be helpful if you are trying to ascertain which pole the person prefers.

That said, if groups or individuals have a lot of energy around one of the overuses and can populate it very quickly and robustly and then talk wistfully of the opposite benefits, it could very likely be a sign that they are experiencing the overuses of the first quadrant. They know the "pain" well and can populate the quadrant without much thought, while the opposite benefits seem like a lovely answer to their situation.

Another point illustrated by this case is the power of using the diagonals as a resource. Because it can be so difficult to see the full extent of the overuses of our preferred pole, it is helpful to use the opposites on the diagonal as a way to paint a fuller picture of the interdependent dynamic. As pointed out before, we don't recommend starting by simply transferring the opposites to the other diagonal. It's most helpful to fill out the map by talking about each quadrant separately and then going back and "checking your math" by examining the opposites.

A final point illustrated by this case is that emotions and the heart are often at the center of conversations in the Transformational Third Way and Vulnerability Throughway. Standing in the Third Way requires that we find a way to be OK with the tension between the poles and may require an identity shift. Mapping the benefits and overuses helps people make sense of the data and see themselves and others more fully. Exploring the Transformational Third Way and Vulnerability Throughway can help people, over time, learn to hold and ultimately resolve the contradiction in themselves — making transformation possible.

Organizational Structure—Stopping the Pendulum Swing and Engaging Stakeholders

Background

CKR was an organization that worked to match large government agencies and contractors with appropriate software solutions. Since the inception of the company, the organization had been structured so that different teams (sales, support, marketing, etc.) were organized along vendor or provider lines. These teams represented, sold, and supported certain products and solutions in the portfolio.

The organization was very successful, but over time, complaints began to surface:

- There was a lack of flexibility meeting client demands because of loyalty to vendors.

- The CKR brand was limited — customers associated CKR with specific software products, not as a service provider or problem-solving partner.

- CKR was missing out on opportunities to cross sell because departments/teams didn't have insight into what others were doing.

As frustration grew, the Executive Leadership Team (ELT) decided, at the lead of the CEO, to take action and "solve these issues" by restructuring the organization. Not surprisingly, some ELT members were resistant to reorganizing, while others were enthusiastic about the prospect. Even so, the CEO scheduled a planning retreat to hammer out the details of the new structure and a team was put in place to craft the agenda and details of the event. While everything looked good on the surface, behind the scenes the camp of resistors was planning how to thwart the reorganization conversation.

In the midst of planning, the team designing the offsite (which included two of the resistors) was introduced to polarities and created a quick and high-level map to understand how the "problems" they were trying to solve were actually the downsides of a polarity. The discussion illuminated how "solving" these issues with the reorg the ELT was considering would simply result in swinging the pendulum to achieve the opposite benefits, which would eventually become just as problematic as they turned to overuses. As a result, the design team decided to introduce the concept of polarities to the entire ELT and to use the lens as a way to deal with the issues that were driving the desire for reorganization. Unfortunately, due to a short planning window, stakeholders such as team leads, vendor representatives, and customer representatives were not able to be included in the offsite.

Mapping

At the beginning of the ELT retreat, the CEO discussed the reasons they had come together—to solve the issues identified above and to work on the prospect of a reorganization. After a short introduction to polarities, which included an overview and a practice mapping of Work::Leisure, the team began exploring Vendor Centric::Client Centric and created the map simplified in Figure 4.4 [page 110]. It quickly became apparent that swinging the pendulum was not the solution they were seeking and that an entire reorg wasn't the right approach.

During the conversation, the resistance of those against the initially proposed reorg (those who held the Vendor Centric diagonal) quickly diminished (relatively speaking). Their point of view was validated and those who held the Client Centric diagonal (including the CEO) spent more time listening, appreciating the upsides of the Vendor Centric pole and acknowledging the potential overuses of their own pole. As a result of valuing the wisdom in the resistance, the team was able to develop and implement a sustainable and successful solution.

One key voice missing from the offsite was that of the stakeholders mentioned above. Because of the vital role they play in creating a map, the group decided to vet the map with these other key groups to ensure they hadn't missed any crucial elements, and to get suggestions for other potential action steps. After doing so, the ELT met again to decide which strategies they would implement in the organization. To monitor the ongoing progress of navigating the polarity, the ELT decided they would revisit the Navigator twice a year to discuss which of the benefits and overuses they were experiencing.

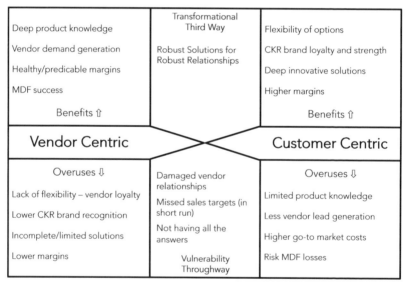

Figure 4.4: Vendor Centric::Client Centric

Takeaways

There are two key takeaways from this case: Importance of stakeholders and wisdom in the resistance. The process of including stakeholders here was done in a way that might seem a bit unconventional to some. Stakeholders were not in the room for the discussion, did not help create the initial map, nor help define any of the strategies. However, because the ELT knew how important these stakeholders were to the process, they actively sought out their voices and views on the work that had been done. This ultimately added several important pieces to the Navigator and impacted overall success.

Secondly, understanding that when a polarity is at play, there is always wisdom in the resistance. This is a big shift for change efforts in organizations. In this case, the "resistance" came to the offsite ready for a bit of a fight, and those advocating for the reorganization were just as prepared to fight back. This isn't surprising or unusual. Having camps take sides and prepare for a fight has wasted countless resources and vast amounts of energy in organizations throughout history. The mapping process in this case allowed the ELT to see the wisdom in the resistance, which was attempting to protect the benefits of the current pole (Vendor Centric). The polarity conversation showed that both diagonals were accurate but that neither was complete and that ultimate success would depend on knowing how to successfully navigate both. The discussion about the vulnerability needed to stand in the Third Way allowed both sides to be heard and for the group to collectively own the risks that were driving their fear of an integrated solution.

Framing a Change Effort—Expand Without Losing

Background

One necessity of being a successful and sustainable organization is the ability to Preserve the Core::Stimulate Progress. While vital, navigating this polarity does not come naturally to all organizations, and for some, it must be an intentional effort. Such was the case with NDOCA, an international association that offered a specific line of products and services to their member base.

Because of the financial crisis and other changes in the industry, it became increasingly obvious that NDOCA needed to change the way it operated in order to stay relevant and best serve its members. As a result, leaders in the organization began to talk of the need to innovate and expand into several very different and resource-heavy lines of products and services. A natural tension arose with some people seeing the new suggestions as the only way forward, while others contended that the resource drain would divert focus and impact the quality of their traditional value to members. As the tension mounted, relationships became strained and the "innovators," as they called themselves, began finding ways to work around those they called the "deadwood." Or, as the other side put it, the "crazies" started to work around "those of us who really care about the members."

The president knew that NDOCA needed change but also wanted to avoid any additional infighting and distraction from mission. Because of her past experiences with polarities, she decided to use the lens to help the organization understand that while they did, in fact, need to do some things radically differently, they would also need to ensure the key services provided to members did not suffer in the process. As a result, she created a plan to pull together her senior team, several representatives from the various departments, and a few key NDOCA members to create a plan to move the organization toward the Third Way.

Mapping

Over the course of several meetings, the group created a Navigator of Preserve Our Core::Stimulate Progress like the one in Figure 4.5 on the following page and identified a path forward. To monitor the polarity over time, the president decided to share the map with the board of directors and to bring the planning team together quarterly to check in on the polarity and the progression of the plan. Department heads also committed to share the Navigator with their teams and to use it as they created future plans for their areas of responsibility.

A key way in which the planning team used polarities was in creating the communication strategy for announcing the shift in the NDOCA's focus. Many organizational change efforts are communicated on one diagonal of the map. Messages outline the problem (the overuses they are currently getting) and lay out the plan to get the solution (the opposite benefits). If NDOCA had made this mistake, it might have sounded like: *Our value to members is diminishing and we are losing them to other organizations, so we are going to focus on developing innovative products and services that attract more members and ensure our longevity.* A communication strategy set up on this perspective would have simultaneously excited some people (those that held the "Stimulate Progress" diagonal) while eliciting resistance from others (those that held the "Preserve the Core" diagonal).

NDOCA used the Polarity Navigator as the backbone for a different communication strategy. Their key message, and eventual rallying cry, became: *We are going to increase our value to members by developing dynamic and innovative new products and services without losing focus on our traditional offerings or sacrificing the quality that our members have come to expect.* This messaging created a different focus in the organization. The key was the *"without losing…or sacrificing…"* element. As a result, the organization was clear that it was not swinging a pendulum but instead going after the benefits of the Stimulate Progress pole without losing the benefits of the Preserve the Core pole that had served them to that point.

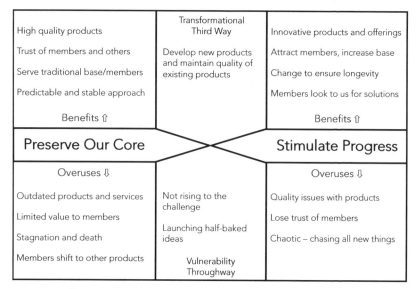

	Transformational Third Way	
High quality products		Innovative products and offerings
Trust of members and others	Develop new products and maintain quality of existing products	Attract members, increase base
Serve traditional base/members		Change to ensure longevity
Predictable and stable approach		Members look to us for solutions
Benefits ⇧		Benefits ⇧
Preserve Our Core		**Stimulate Progress**
Overuses ⇩		Overuses ⇩
Outdated products and services	Not rising to the challenge	Quality issues with products
Limited value to members		Lose trust of members
Stagnation and death	Launching half-baked ideas	Chaotic – chasing all new things
Members shift to other products		
	Vulnerability Throughway	

Figure 4.5: Preserve Our Core::Stimulate Progress

Takeaways

The first important thing about this case is that Figure 4.5, as you might have noticed, is not a textbook map. The Third Way is much more "doing" than "being" and it has unequal items in the benefits and overuses. Some might argue that it shouldn't be in a "how to" book. That's exactly the point. While perfect maps are nice, the more important thing is to use the map to help groups make sense of the paradoxical tension at play in the system. The dialogue that happens as a result of the map is the key to understanding and movement.

The second takeaway is in how the organization used the map to help guide the key messaging surrounding the transition. Framing change efforts as "We need more X *without losing* Y" can lower resistance and increase innovation. For this reason, many practitioners who use the Polarity Navigator refer to it as a tool that helps with continuity-and-change efforts. Chapter 6 has more on this topic.

Several of the cases above require using the Navigator with groups. The section below outlines several important tips to remember when helping a group make sense of a polarity.

Working with and Facilitating Groups

There are multiple facilitation techniques that can be used when working with polarities in groups. If you are a facilitator, you should use any facilitation methods that suit your purposes. Many approaches will be outlined and discussed in future books in this series, but it's worth highlighting a few points here to answer some of the common questions about working with groups and polarities.

Have a Shared Visual

When working with a group, it's important to have a shared visual so the group can create a common Navigator and everyone can feel some ownership in the process. This can be done on a whiteboard or flip charts that can later be transcribed to a proper Navigator. Although projecting a version of the Navigator on a screen and capturing data real time can work, it sometimes stifles the natural flow of thinking as many people see things that are "typed up" as complete or set in stone. We find that writing on surfaces that look less formalized keeps people in a more creative space.

Move to Populate the Benefits and Overuses

Our experience with groups, and the data from our research, suggests that moving as a group can be a vital piece to helping people understand a polarity. One way to do this, when space allows, is to put flip-chart paper in four "corners" of a room for each of the benefits and overuses. Then, as a group, move through the quadrants to populate the benefits and overuses of the map. It can be helpful to move in the direction of the energy flow of the polarity, that is, from the overuses to the diagonal benefits and from the benefits to the corresponding overuses. In an ideal world, we lay out a Navigator on the floor using masking tape to give people a way to actually stand in, and experience, each of the spaces of the map.

Alternatively, when working with a larger group, break into two to four smaller groups and have each group start at a different flip chart. Give them a bit of time, no more than two minutes, to populate that quadrant. Do not let them spend too long; you do not want them to exhaust all of the possibilities in that quadrant. Then move the groups in the direction of the energy flow until all groups have contributed to each set of benefits and overuses. A possible creative addition to help get people out of their heads is to have groups in the last round draw an image to capture the essence of that quadrant. This is a great way to give people a different way to see and make sense of the dynamic.

As an aside, you can often tell, or diagnose, a group's preferences and diagonals by paying attention to the length of the lists they create and the energy they have in discussing each of the quadrants. If they have long lists in two diagonal quadrants, it could be a sign they hold that point of view — that they prefer that diagonal way of seeing the world. Additionally, paying attention to the energy a group has when discussing each of the quadrants can often provide good insight into their current relationship to the polarity.

Reach Agreement and Understanding

Regardless of the method you use to populate the map, when finished, take the flip charts from each quadrant and hang them on one wall on either side of the flipcharts for the Third Way and Throughway in order to create a Navigator that everyone can see. Begin by simply asking the group, "What do you see?" Then have the group consider, discuss, and edit the benefits and overuses as needed. Use the techniques from the Values Clarification section [page 65] in Chapter 3 to help the group deepen their understanding of their less-preferred diagonal.

Create a Touchstone Third Way

After exploring the benefits and overuses, move to the Transformational Third Way and the Vulnerability Throughway. Begin by brainstorming possible descriptions of the Third Way using the types of questions presented throughout this book, and eventually move the group to agreement. This can be done as a large group or in subgroups. Remember that the words used to label the Third Way only have to make sense to the group. There is likely to be no single, existing word for it (remember the nut and bolt), so the terminology will be unique—typically a short phrase, metaphor, or a made-up word. It simply has to be a shorthand and touchstone for the group to quickly remember the harmonization of the poles—the new, unique tone containing both poles yet diminishing neither.

When discussing a possible Third Way, be prepared for some of the ideas to be more like strategies. If this happens, capture them as *potential* strategies (tell the group you'll come back to those) and redirect the group to focus on what mindset or experience of being in the Third Way would drive that action using the tips in Chapter 3 on More Being, Less Doing [page 72].

Name Collective and Individual Vulnerabilities

The Vulnerability Throughway is a bit more nuanced. When working with groups, it is helpful to have two levels of conversation. The first is about what feels risky at the group level, and the second is about the individuals and their personal vulnerabilities. Because this can be a more revealing conversation than those thus far in the process, it is helpful to begin the first discussion with a bit of quiet reflection, moving to partner or trio conversations, and finally moving to the entire group. Use good facilitation techniques to draw out, and dig into, the vulnerability the group needs to step into as they stand in the Third Way. In addition to using any of the concepts and ideas suggested throughout the book for exploring the Vulnerability Throughway, you can also follow this process:

- Have each person in the group stand (or imagine they are standing) in the comfort of their preferred diagonal.
- Invite them to step off of their diagonal into the Third Way, pausing to notice any discomfort or tension.
- Ask them to step into the Vulnerability Throughway and explore any of the following questions:
  - What is at stake if you step into the Third Way?
  - What is the potential cost of navigating from the Third Way?
  - What feels risky about holding both poles together?

Regardless of how you explore the vulnerability, remember that any "how will we do that" ideas should be captured as potential strategies to be revisited.

After discussing the vulnerability required of the group, have individuals reflect on what would be risky for them, personally, as the group is called to stand in the Third Way. Depending on your facilitation goals, you can have people share as partners, subgroups, or in the large group about the vulnerability they'll personally be stepping into. In some groups, it can be helpful to capture each person's response in the Vulnerability Throughway so that the group can support one another as they move forward. Regardless of how it is done, this is an important step for the group to navigate the Individual::Group polarity. Focusing only on the vulnerabilities of the group while neglecting the individual is only half of the picture!

Brainstorm Possible Actions

Finally, move to strategies. We find it helpful to start with brainstorming a list of potential strategies to 1) stand in the Third Way, 2) manage and stay with the vulnerability, and 3) monitor the polarity over time. Be sure to draw on the tips for creating strategies from earlier in the book. It's best to tee this up as a brainstorming session—capture the ideas, making it clear to the group that, at this point, they are not coming to agreement. Then use basic facilitation techniques to bring the group to agreement about strategies that are actionable and trackable. Once finalized, the actions can be transferred to the Navigator.

Movement Is Key

You'll notice here that movement of the group (and when working with individuals) is incredibly powerful. Physically moving as a group through the Navigator not only supports the group in experiencing the dynamic and developing an understanding of their relationship to it, it also allows each individual within the group to surface insights, access data, and listen to the wisdom the body has to offer—insights the head alone may not have access to. To navigate a polarity from the Third Way, we have to learn to not only make sense of the dynamic, we have to learn to embody it. Thankfully, when we engage the whole body in this work, it can lead the head to the heart, serving as the ultimate guide to the Third Way.

Conclusion

The cases and tips above provide a brief window into how to use polarities in a variety of situations and several of the key advantages to doing so. The follow-up books in this series examine cases like these in more depth—some deal with various sectors and types of organizations, while others deal with specific polarities. These books will allow for much more Breadth::Depth than we can provide here.

Regardless of the organization or issue, most polarity engagements follow a specified set of steps to guide the process, outlined here simply as Analyze, Map, Act, and Monitor. We suggest adding a step to Connect people to the Third Way and the vulnerability it takes to sustain it. There are other approaches outlined in other books in the series. The key is to find a process that helps the group, organization, or individual you are working with to make sense of the polarity and then act to navigate it effectively. While the most uncomfortable of the steps is Connect, the most difficult of the steps is Analyze—knowing whether or not the situation is a polarity to manage or simply a problem to solve. The next chapter takes a deep dive into this topic and provides some potentially helpful tips.

In Summary:

There are five steps to navigating a polarity:

1. **Analyze to See** whether it is a problem or polarity
2. **Map to Understand** the benefits and overuses of each pole
3. **Explore to Connect** by experiencing the Third Way and vulnerability
4. **Act to Expand** by creating strategies and actions
5. **Monitor to Discern** how the polarity is being navigated over time

This process can be used with any level of system—individual, group, organization, family, or community.

CHAPTER 5

SEEING POLARITIES

One of the most common responses people have after learning about polarities is: *This all makes sense, and I understand how to do a Navigator, but how do you know if something is a polarity to navigate or just a problem to solve?* It's understandable because "seeing" is one of the most difficult and yet most important aspects of working with polarities. In this chapter, we'll outline several tips and tricks to tell the difference between problems that require either/or thinking and polarities that call us to think both/and.

Before doing so, it's worth underscoring the importance of either/or thinking. The role the either/or mindset plays in our ability to function in the world is invaluable. If a piano is dropping on your head, you can *either* stand there *or* run out of the way—hopefully quickly. When you get a job offer, you can decide to *either* accept it *or* reject it. If you take it, you can decide to *either* drive *or* take the train to work. When you find out your boss is embezzling money, you can decide to *either* stay put *or* look for a new job. We need and benefit from either/or thinking.

It's also important not to confuse either/or thinking with simplicity. The world is filled with complex problems that require us to make either/or choices as we move toward resolution. Putting humans on Mars will require many either/or problems to be solved. Managing a global supply chain of refrigerated vaccines in 34 countries is a complex problem that relies on an either/or mindset for success. Therefore, focusing only on both/and thinking, making it somehow superior to either/or thinking and suggesting that it is the best way of approaching the world, is actually a form of either/or thinking! That said, knowing how to distinguish between each and being able to analyze a situation to determine if, and how, there is a polarity at play is a vital skill, for only then can we have any hope of navigating it effectively.

Do We Need to See All Polarities?

As we dive into how to distinguish polarity situations from other situations, it's important to reiterate: Not everything is a polarity, and not all polarities are worth taking the time to map because we are likely already navigating them well. For example, waking up every morning and creating a Navigator of Inhale::Exhale probably isn't necessary because, if you're like the majority of living beings, you naturally understand the dynamic and navigate it well over time.

Take another example involving two leaders, Sheree and Audrey. Audrey organizes her team in a way that harmonizes Structure::Flexibility. She sets expectations and guidelines that can shift when needed. Audrey seems naturally wired to effectively navigate this tension without much thought. Audrey's leadership challenge, however, is that she can't hold her tongue and doesn't hesitate when it comes to telling people what's on her mind (thereby getting the overuses of Candor). Sheree, on the other hand, instinctively knows how to tell people her honest thoughts in a way that maintains and even strengthens the relationship. Unlike Audrey, she naturally leverages Candor::Diplomacy. However, she's unlike Audrey when it comes to Structure::Flexibility. Sheree has a difficult time implementing the right processes on her team, and she allows people too much flexibility in how they approach their work, which creates a bit of chaos. Her team's effectiveness is hindered by the overuses of Flexibility. In this example, Sheree would benefit from creating a Navigator to intentionally harmonize Structure::Flexibility, while it wouldn't be worth the time mapping Candor::Diplomacy because she navigates that dynamic so naturally. Audrey is just the opposite. Not all polarities are worth being mapped by everyone.

To determine if a polarity is worth paying attention to, it can be helpful to ask any of the following questions:

- *To what degree might this polarity limit my overall effectiveness if I don't navigate it more effectively?*
- *Am I, or my team, Suffering Paradox, and would navigating increase our effectiveness?*
- *To what degree does ignoring this dynamic put our overall success at risk?*

The answers will help you decide how much, if any, attention you should give to the polarity. Of course, before you can do that, you have to be able to identify if, when, and how a polarity might be at play in any situation. This is a difficult muscle to build but, over time, if you use the lenses laid out below, it becomes natural to see the polarities in the situations and dynamics of any system.

Analyze to See—Is it a Problem or a Polarity?

Take Action to Pause

Before exploring specific tips for spotting polarities, remember, the most effective way to build the muscle of spotting polarities is to create the habit of simply pausing when in a problematic situation and asking, *"Could there be a polarity here?"* We are wired to jump to action, and many of us are experts at doing it quickly! When faced with any issue, simply taking the time to consider whether or not it is a polarity is a crucial step. Developing the ability to pause to analyze, therefore, is a great skill in seeing polarities.

Remember the three Ps: Facing a Problem...take a Pause...is it a Polarity?

Places to Look for Polarities

The seven types of situations outlined below are places that polarities are frequently found. While the list is not exhaustive, these tend to be the most helpful for people seeking to develop an eye for polarities as they analyze problematic situations. There's likely a polarity at play when you notice:

- From-To Situations
- Too Much of a Good Thing
- Opposite Arguments
- Fear of Taking it Too Far
- Threat of Losing Identity
- The "Other" is a Villain
- The Energy is Stuck

From-To Situations

You're likely dealing with a polarity if: You are in a situation in which there is a desire to swing *from* one way of being *to* another. This is one of Johnson's criteria[1] worth highlighting here because it is probably the most common way to recognize a polarity situation. For example, "We need to go *from* cutting corners and buying cheap parts *to* getting customers a product they're satisfied with that won't fall apart in three months."

In many, if not most, From-To situations, there is a desire to move from the overuses of one pole to the benefits of the other. In the case of the example above, you would be moving from the overuse of Focus on Costs (cutting corners, cheap parts) to the benefits of Focus on Quality (customer satisfaction, products that last). The From-To dynamic underlies several of the "places to look" outlined below, and numerous examples have been highlighted throughout this book. When you are in a From-To situation, consider these things to help identify the polarity:

- Is the "From" state (or part of it) the result of focusing on or having too much of something? If so, what? *We're in this situation because we are too* _____?
  - Look at a list of polarities for ideas of poles. Ask which of them the "From" state might be the overuse of.
- Is the "To" state (or part of it) the benefit, or upside, of a pole? If so, what? *These things would result from us being more* _____?
  - Look at a list of polarities for ideas of poles. Ask which of them might elicit the attraction to the "To" state.

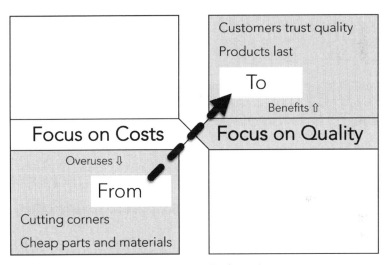

Figure 5.1: From-To Situations

Too Much of a Good Thing

You're likely dealing with a polarity if: The problem you're encountering is a result of overdoing something you're really good at, or really value, and the adage "too much of a good thing" or "a strength becomes a weakness" rings in your ears. When a system or individual highly values something, there is a chance they will over-focus on it and begin to experience its

126 NAVIGATING POLARITIES

downsides. Additionally, when one part of the system starts to complain about the "problems" being experienced (the overuses), there is typically a reaction to those complaints from people who value the pole being overused.

Take the example of a sales organization that values, and is good at, Competition. Because they love this pole so much, they over-focus on it and begin to experience problems of cutthroat behavior, team members being isolated from one another, and a lack of camaraderie (the overuses of Competition). When several people begin to complain and suggest that things need to change, those who value the competitive environment and the benefits it brings react negatively to the comments and see those concerned about the situation as whiners. In cases like this, people are usually unaware their reaction is the result of a value being stepped on and will have trouble seeing, or will choose to deny, there are issues. If you are in a situation where you have too much of a good thing, the polarity might become clear by considering the following points.

- Think about the issues and complaints. Are they the result of overdoing something you're really good at or you really value? What is it? Could it be the pole of a polarity?

- If people react negatively or defensively when discussing an issue, could it be that something they value is being threatened? What's important to them that brings good things, but that the system might be getting too much of? Could it be the pole of a polarity?

Opposite Arguments

You're likely dealing with a polarity if: There are two sides to an argument, and the positive aspects of one option are the exact opposites of the negative aspects of the other. For example, Denise thinks they should do it her way because "the process will be faster with a single point person" and contends that "if we do it Sheila's way, the process will be laborious with too many cooks in the kitchen and no one in charge." Sheila, however, says, "Doing it my way will create buy-in to the solutions whereas Denise's approach will leave people feeling like the solutions are being imposed upon them."

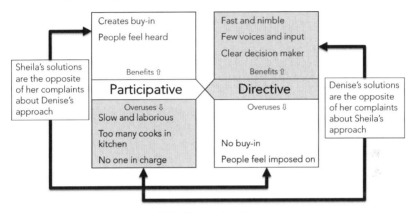

Figure 5.2: Opposite Arguments

In this situation, each prefers their solution because the "pros" of their approach outweigh the seeming "cons" of the other. In actuality, these are not pros and cons but rather benefits and overuses of a polarity. Each person's proposed solutions are essentially the benefits of the pole they value, which are the exact opposites of the problems they anticipate from the other person's approach (that pole's overuses). When this is the case, step back and consider that each argument might be the result of seeing on a diagonal and not looking at the entire polarity. These questions might help:

- Are the benefits of Approach A the opposite of the problems created by Approach B, and vice versa? If so, does Approach A, if taken too far, have downsides that would be addressed or alleviated by Approach B?

- Does each argument, if taken to an extreme, have overuses—not cons, but downsides that result from taking the solution too far?

Fear of Taking it Too Far

You're likely dealing with a polarity if: What's being proposed will "be OK in the short term, but we'll have to be careful not to take it too far." This concern might arise because the proposal is actually the benefit of a pole, and some people (usually those who prefer the current pole) can already see the potential overuses to the solution.

For example, imagine an organization filled with excitement because of an announcement that it will implement a flexible work schedule to allow people more autonomy in how, when, and where they work because this will help people feel empowered and engaged. There are several managers who are excited, but also a bit torn, saying things like, "I think this'll be good, but we'll need to keep an eye on it because I'm afraid it could lead to a bit of chaos and us not knowing what's going on" and "I'm supportive, overall, but concerned people will start taking advantage of it and we'll have situations where people are inaccessible and not producing what's required."

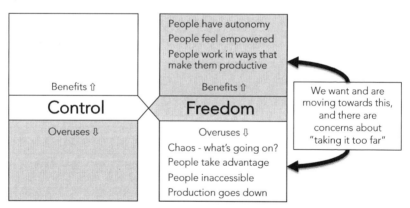

Figure 5.3: Taking it Too Far

If these arguments are valid repercussions of taking the solution too far, then there's a strong probability a polarity is at play under the proposed initiative. In those cases, consider these questions:

- Listen to the concerns. At their root, are they about taking the proposed solution too far—having too much of it? If so, are the concerns the overuses of a potential pole—what is it?

- If the root of the concern seems to be about "taking it too far," ask yourself: Based on their concern, which values of theirs would be at risk? These could be the benefits of a pole—what is it?

Threat of Losing Identity

You're likely dealing with a polarity if: There is a desire to begin doing something new but doing so seems to threaten things you value or benefits *you already have*. In other words, doing more of "the new thing" means sacrificing something currently of value. The key here is: *one option threatens benefits you already have*.

While this happens at all levels of systems, on an individual level it might look something like this: "If I spend more time connecting with people and bringing them along in the process, then I'll lose my ability to move things quickly. People respect my laser-focus on the finish line—it's what I'm known for." In this case, the benefits of one pole (Focus on Relationship) seem to threaten the benefits of the other (Focus on Task). When a polarity like this is approached with an either/or mindset, it appears as if obtaining the upsides of one pole requires giving up, or losing, the benefits of the other.

Reframing the situation as a polarity leads to greater effectiveness by showing both can be possible. When faced with situations where "doing X will threaten Y," consider these questions to help determine if there is a polarity:

- What might X be the benefits of, and does the approach have potential overuses? If these overuses are the opposites of Y (the things being threatened), then it's probably a polarity. What is Y the upside of?

- Are X and Y the potential benefits of two different poles? If so, what might they be?

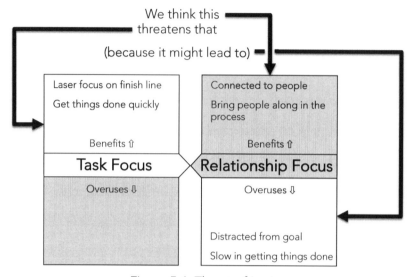

Figure 5.4: Threat of Losing

The Other is a Villain

You're likely dealing with a polarity if: There is an "other" — another person, side, or group — and they are being demonized and viewed as roadblocks, or their approach is seen as having no value. The theory of Suffering Paradox suggests that when caught in a paradoxical tension, we need, or create, an "other" to help us validate and make sense of our point of view. Since we tend to see those who prefer the opposite pole in terms of their overuses, and not in terms of their benefits, it becomes very easy to make the "other" wrong. In a polarity situation, the overuses of the "other's" pole threaten the values we hold dear (the benefits of our pole), and in an effort to protect our values, we are drawn to fight the attacker. It's seductive at that point to make them the villain in our drama.

This might sound like, "Ali's group is terrible...they just keep us spinning and prevent us from making any forward progress...

they just want to talk about possibilities and never lock down a plan of action...we're the only ones who really want to get a product out the door. Just stick to a plan already!" (see Figure 5.5 on the following page). Or, "I am so fed up with the way Santo's group keeps excluding people from the decisions. They say they want things done quickly, but what they really want is to be secretive and control what's going on."

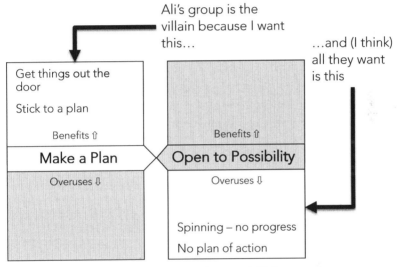

Figure 5.5: Other is a Villain

This is easy to spot in politics around the globe. Using the US as an example, it's not uncommon to hear, "Blue States are filled with radical liberals who want to take away my freedoms and give tons of handouts to the slackers. The Socialists!" This is often retorted by "Oh, yeah, Red States are heartless, greedy, and narrow-minded. They only care about themselves—Capitalist Pigs!" When people are demonizing another person or group, consider these points to determine if there is a polarity at play:

- Take the complaints about "the other" and then consider the exact opposite of each. Do these opposites represent the values of the one doing the demonizing? If so, what pole could the complaints be the overuse of? And what pole could the values be the benefits of?

- Is the "other" being demonized because they, in some way, threaten the values of the party doing the demonizing? What are those values, and what pole might they be the benefits of? To get a good sense of the values, you can ask the person doing the demonizing, "So, what important thing is put at risk because of 'their' viewpoint or their approach?"

The Energy is Stuck

You *might* be dealing with a polarity if: Two "sides" have been pushing against each other for so long the energy in the system has come to a standstill and no real progress is being made. This often results from, or is coupled with, demonizing the "other." If a group sees only from the perspective of their diagonal and pushes things in that direction and then encounters a group pushing along the opposite diagonal, the energy can get stuck in the middle and a stalemate occurs with nothing getting done in the system. When a system is stuck and progress is slow and laborious at best, it is an indicator that a polarity might be at play. Take the Red State–Blue State example above and then think about the stuck energy in the US Congress.

These "stuck" symptoms are often palpable and can sound like, "Good luck trying to get that done; they'll fight you tooth and nail because all they care about is overengineering the process to the point that it strangles everything." Or "He's impossible to work with—he doesn't appreciate that holding people accountable for deliverables is the only way to move things through the pipeline—we've just stopped talking about it altogether." If you're in a situation that seems stuck and you are trying to determine if it's a polarity, consider these questions:

- At its core, is the argument, or the reason people are stuck, about things they value? What core principles are driving the viewpoints of each side? Are these values the benefits of different poles?

- After listening to complaints about the "other," you can ask: *If we went totally in their direction and did things their way, what would we risk? What's important that would be threatened?* If people respond with things that are the opposite of their original complaints about the "other," you can set them on a diagonal to identify the polarity.

Polarities Under Problems

Sometimes, when analyzing situations to determine if they are a problem or a polarity, they can appear to be both—there is a problem on the surface with one or more polarities underneath it. Here are a few examples:

- You have to decide whether to contract with Vendor A or Vendor B. Vendor A is known for speed and Vendor B has a reputation for quality. On the surface, this is a problem to solve—the choices are not interdependent, and the situation will not be ongoing. However, there could be polarities under the problem worth paying attention to over time. If you select Vendor A because speed is your main focus, even though Vendor B has better quality, and you continue to use speed as the criteria by which you select all vendors in the future, you might eventually experience the overuses of Focus on Speed in the Focus on Speed::Focus on Quality polarity.

- An employee misses a deadline. A report was supposed to be finished by noon, but the manager doesn't receive it until the following morning. The manager now has a problem: Do they say something about the missed deadline or let it slide? While it makes sense in the moment to treat this either/or situation like a problem, there is a polarity under it that needs to be navigated over time. A manager who always "lets it slip" and never says anything when employees miss a target will eventually get the overuses of Unconditional Respect and miss out on the benefits of Conditional Respect.

In both instances, the key to determining whether or not to be concerned about the polarity under the problem has to do with the factor "over time." Consider the first scenario. If the situation is a one-time or very rare occurrence like designing a website, for instance, the Speed::Quality polarity might not warrant concern. Only if it's a situation in which you are repeatedly choosing different vendors over an extended period of time might the polarity need to be paid attention to more closely. "Over time" is a key indicator when dealing with situations that contain a problem with polarities underneath it.

Practice Pausing

If there's a problem, pause.

Identifying polarities is not easy. Especially given that situations containing polarities can quickly trigger emotional responses for everyone involved. Couple that with time pressure and a drive for action, and it's no wonder people have a hard time seeing the polarities around them. The tips in this chapter can be useful lenses as you search for polarities, but the real key is pausing to simply ask the question: Could there be a polarity here?

Facing a Problem…take a Pause…is there a Polarity? Without the pause, building the muscle of seeing polarities is extremely difficult. But if individuals and systems develop the habit of including "Could there be a polarity here?" as one of the questions used during any problem-definition stage, seeing polarities becomes almost second nature. Pausing is the platform upon which the tips in this chapter become useful and serves to ensure that we have them and they don't have us.

In Summary:

It's wise to look for a polarity when you notice:

- From-To Situations—there's a push from one pole's overuses to the other pole's benefits
- Too Much of a Good Thing—the current situation exists from taking a strength too far (into its overuses)
- Opposite Arguments—the positive points of Argument A are opposite of the negative points of Argument B and vice versa
- Fear of Taking it Too Far—people are concerned the proposed solution (the benefits of the other pole) will swing too far and lead to undesirable results (the other pole's overuses)
- Threat of Losing Identity—concern that what I value (the benefits of my preferred pole) or who I am might be diminished if I start doing "that" (the benefits of the other pole)
- The "Other" is a Villain—another person or group is going after, or creating, the opposite of what we want, so we demonize and make them wrong
- The Energy is Stuck—two groups are virtually deadlocked, each pushing or pulling in a different direction such that nothing is getting done

The most helpful way to recognize a polarity is to practice pausing. Facing a problem...take a pause...is it a polarity?

CHAPTER 6

POLARITIES AND IMPACT

This introductory book outlines the nature of polarities, how to use the Polarity Navigator as a sensemaking tool to navigate them, and practical tips on how to see the dynamic at play in different situations. In this final chapter, we'll discuss how to use polarities as a way to gain personal or organizational awareness and how polarities can be a resource for change efforts and driving different conversations in the world.

We navigate polarities more easily and more effectively when we, and those we work with, pay attention to Be::Do — who we *be* as much as what we *do*. Navigating this polarity of Be::Do requires us to constantly develop three faculties central to working with polarities at any level of system. Doing so puts us in a better position to effectively deal with the tensions of any paradox we might be suffering. These faculties are outlined below.

Awareness, Acceptance, and Action

Awareness illuminates. Becoming more conscious of our diagonals and the sensations, feelings, and habits of mind associated with them is key to effectively navigating polarities. Awareness allows for an expansiveness that helps us see and relate to ourselves and others more completely. It is experienced when we bring our full attention to the moment and what's really going on for us. When we are willing to look at ourselves, we begin to see attachment, reactivity, fear, a desire for certainty, and the root causes of Suffering Paradox. Suffering is the natural consequence of overlooking, or being blind to, a polarity and how we are in it and it is in us. You can build this muscle, and help others do the same, by pausing to ask questions like:

- What's my relationship to this polarity?
- What diagonal do I naturally hold? How strong is my attachment to it?
- In what ways is part of "who I am" defined by a pole of this polarity?
- How attached am I to one of the poles and the benefits it brings?

Seeking, and being open to, feedback in these areas is another way to illuminate our relationship with the polarity. No matter the method, increasing our awareness of our diagonal will always help us Navigate Paradox more effectively.

Acceptance unlocks. No matter what we discover, we need to be able to allow it all in—all of the thoughts, emotions, and tensions associated with our preferences and the dynamic of a polarity. Acceptance is a loving act done with an open heart. Judgment doesn't benefit us here; we can't punish ourselves for our attachment to a pole, or others for theirs. It has served us well—to a point. We are now just encountering the overuse. Like awareness, acceptance is experienced when we bring our full attention to the moment and sit with a deep trust of what is. Asking questions like these, without judgment, can help with acceptance:

- In what ways have the benefits of the pole made me/us successful?
- What are the real impacts of the overuses on this situation and the people involved?
- How have the overuses resulted from my desire to ensure I/we get the benefits I value?
- What's at risk if I don't navigate this polarity more effectively?

From this place we can greet reality, the truth of the interdependent pair, and our relationship to it. Acceptance and letting

go show us a path to a place of rest and ease that is always available when we turn toward the resistance rather than turning
away from it or trying to fight it.

Action moves. When we have the fortitude to stand with
the tension and move forward in a more complete way, transformation is possible. Frank Ostaseski[1] suggests that when fear
speaks, courageous action is the heart's answer. Courageous
action sustains us in the face of paradoxical tension. It helps us
risk the known of our diagonal for the unknown of the Third
Way and be present with the powerful states of mind and heart
in the Vulnerability Throughway. It allows us to negotiate choice
points — stepping into the vulnerability rather than away from it,
opening up rather than armoring up, developing new ways of
seeing, being, and behaving rather than defaulting to the status
quo. Action is the call to courage that invites us to choose love
over fear.

When we are able to be *and* do awareness, acceptance, and
action, we invite others to do the same. Through this, we create
the space for individuals, teams, and organizations to reduce suffering and reap the rewards of navigating polarities.

Polarities Scale to All Level of Systems

It's likely become clear by this point that many polarities are
relevant across multiple levels of systems. For instance, Structure::Flexibility looks very similar for parents, leaders, teachers,
nonprofits, teams, societies, and likely any other system you
can think of. The same holds true for polarities such as Stability::Change, Task::Relationship, Focus on the Part::Focus on the
Whole, and countless others.

When this is the case, the things we learn and the ways in
which we apply the polarity can scale across the systems as well.
This is why someone who doesn't know anything about a team's
specific struggle with Structure::Flexibility can understand and

speak to that struggle—because we've all experienced it in one form or another. Although the experience of the Third Way, the risks of the Throughway, and the strategies will be unique to the system, most people will have experience navigating, or suffering, the specific polarity dynamic.

Because of this scalability, *the tips and applications below can be used at any level of system*. When we discuss individuals, know that you can also scale the thoughts and ideas to the team, department, or organization level. Likewise, when examining how to use these concepts with a group, know that you can scale the methodology down to apply to the individual level. That's one of the beauties of polarities—they are scalable, they are everywhere, we've all had a lifetime of dealing with them, and we have countless opportunities to learn how to navigate them effectively.

Polarities as an Individual and Organizational Diagnostic

There is no doubt that completing a Navigator helps people make sense of a polarity, and yet, it can sometimes be valuable to have people dig deeper and take a different perspective on the Navigator itself. The methods below can increase awareness and acceptance in the name of moving individuals, groups, and organizations to more sustained action. While not exhaustive, these are several of the ways to use a different lens to interpret the Navigator.

Special note: The keys below are just that, keys. They should be used as an overlay to interpret an already completed Navigator. These are not things to think about when completing a Navigator.

Increasing Awareness

A Navigator can shed light on how a specific polarity plays out in different situations for individuals. While completing the tool can be enlightening and help people move to action, the key below can help individuals see how they are showing up and impacting others, thus setting the stage for true transformation. If a person, team, or organization puts their preferred (natural/default) pole on the left, then the following key can be used to expand awareness, inspire acceptance, and encourage thoughtful action (see Figure 6.1 [page 143]). The items that populate the upper-left quadrant, the benefits of the preferred pole, are things the person *values*. These things drive the person's actions in particular situations because the individual works to bring them into the world. It can be enlightening to explore to what degree these things have been adopted as part of the person's identity. How much of who they see themselves as in the world is connected to the ways in which they strive to bring these values to different situations? There is room for lots of rich exploration here.

Alternately, the bottom right-hand corner, the overuses of the less-preferred pole, are things the person *fears* or doesn't want in the world. The individual will typically work to move situations away from these things. They will often equate these qualities with, and use them to describe, people who prefer that pole. These things can be mined for insight about the Vulnerability Throughway. What is it that feels risky about the things in this quadrant? What kind of discomfort does the person have to be with when the fear of those things raises its head?

The upper right-hand quadrant, where the benefits of the less-preferred pole are listed, is a place of *opportunity or potential* for the individual. These are the things that they probably aren't getting in their life, yet they could if they stood in the Third Way. These may be things the person has said they want to move toward, or have more of, in their life. Additionally, they may have received feedback that they need to "be more of" these things, yet it's been difficult for them to achieve because, if they are like many others, they can't see how to step into this untapped potential without sacrificing the things they value. They think they can be either one or the other, they can't possibly be both. It can be both exciting and a tad stressful to explore these opportunities. Has the person been made aware of them as opportunities in the past? What gets in the way of being, or doing, those things? What benefit would they bring to the person's effectiveness or success?

If it hasn't already become apparent, the items in the bottom-left quadrant, the overuses of the preferred pole, are potential *blind spots* for the individual. The stronger their preference for the pole, the more likely they are demonstrating some of the items in this space—especially to those who do not share their pole preference. It's also possible the person is aware of these overuses and wants to move away from them. This would be a classic example of From-To described in Chapter 5 [page 124] as part of Analyzing to See. This area is one to explore gently, as the person might be unaware of the ways they are showing up and impacting others. Likewise, there could be self-judgment and a framing of the situation as "part of my identity that is bad." Helping the person reframe and see the situation as an overuse of strengths can be particularly helpful. Exploring the long-term costs of these things (potentially) being true can help someone explore the suffering they might be experiencing or that they might be inflicting on others.

Using this key to explore and gain further insights will lead to a richer discussion about the Third Way and Vulnerability Throughway. This increased awareness and acceptance will lead to more sustainable action.

Values and Potential Parts of Identity	Transformational Third Way	Opportunities and Things to Move Towards
• In what ways would these things show up in a description of "Who I am…"? • How highly do I value them? How tightly or loosely are they held? Benefits ⇧		• In what ways would these things add to my effectiveness? • What's the impact if these things are missing? Benefits ⇧
Preferred		Less Preferred
Overuses ⇩ **Potential Blind Spots and Things to Shift** • In what ways might these things be showing up and limiting my effectiveness? • In what ways might I be blind to these things in my life?	Vulnerability Throughway	Overuses ⇩ **Fears and Judgements of Others** • What seems so bad about these – what are the negative impacts I'm afraid of? • What judgement do I have of people who exhibit these qualities?

Figure 6.1: A Key for Increasing Awareness

Another version of this key can be used when working with leaders and can be modified for other levels of system (See Figure 6.2 on following page). Like the overlay above, have the individual complete the Navigator by putting their preferred, or default, pole on the left. After completing the Navigator, use the key below to help the person deepen their awareness and acceptance of their relationship to the polarity. Again, do not use these questions to complete the benefits and overuses. Use it only as a way to help interpret and make more sense of those quadrants.

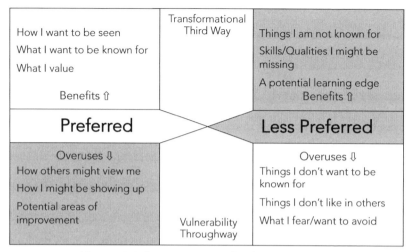

Figure 6.2: Increasing Leadership Awareness

You can explore this key by asking deepening questions like the ones in the previous key.

Increasing Team or Organizational Awareness

Because polarities can be used across all levels of systems, the techniques and keys described in the previous section can also be used for groups or an entire organization. The same types of considerations and questions can be used to increase awareness and acceptance by individuals and the team as they determine strategies to stand in the Third Way.

The Navigator and Change Initiatives

Many, if not most, organizational changes involve polarities. If the change initiative itself is not set up on a diagonal — a move from the overuses of a pole to the benefits of another pole (e.g., Decentralize::Centralize) — then it is likely in response to a problem that has polarities embedded within or underneath it (e.g., implementing a work-from-home policy sits upon the Regulate::Freedom polarity). Because of this, a polarity lens is a great way to increase our understanding of change and evolution in systems and, more importantly, to save time, energy, and resources in our change initiatives.

When a polarity situation is treated as a problem to be solved, there is reduced likelihood of success and an increased likelihood of frustration, damaged morale, and wasted energy. Long-term sustainability is less likely because the solution being proposed is attached to just one pole. For example, the benefits of Centralization eventually become the overuses. As soon as the system begins to encounter the overuses of the new pole, there will be cries to return to the original pole to regain the benefits that were lost as a result of the swing, thus eroding confidence in the leaders who proposed the change to begin with.

This highlights another issue in treating a polarity like a problem—in the long run, the "solution" will look like a mistake and others will likely want to blame those who "messed it up." Continuing the Centralization example above, when the system begins to experience the overuses, problems become readily apparent. As the Sr. Team begins to talk about decentralizing, people in the organization say things like, "They don't know what they're doing, they should've never centralized in the first place" and "They've wasted so much time and money—I can't believe how much they get paid just to mess things up!"

If you mistakenly treat a polarity like a problem, you may gain benefits in the short term, but over time you will most likely experience the cost of overuses. Unfortunately, when that happens, you'll look like you're the one that caused the problems! The solution you proposed wasn't a mistake—it was a logical response to the problems being encountered. It was an accurate assessment, it just wasn't complete. Change efforts created on a diagonal never are, which is why it's important to think of the three Ps when involved in a change: Facing a Problem...take a Pause...is it a Polarity?

Wisdom in the Resistance

One of the most useful ways a polarity lens can aid a change initiative is in how resistance is viewed and engaged. When attempting to move from the overuses of one pole to the benefits of the other, resistance comes from people who hold the other diagonal — who don't want, or fear, the overuses of the pole we're proposing we move toward. The resistance is not necessarily because they don't want the proposed benefits or they think those things aren't a good idea. Instead, people resist a change on the diagonal because they don't want the overuses of the pole the initiative is trying to shift toward. They perceive the change as a threat to the things they value (the benefits of the current pole) because they are convinced they can't have both (See Figure 6.3). The thought of reaping the overuses of the new pole is so uncomfortable they'd rather not go after the benefits at all. It takes vulnerability to step into that space. The mentality is: I'd rather live with the pain of these overuses here (what I know) than experience the pain of those overuses over there (what I don't ever want to know).

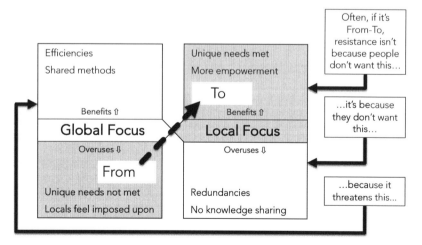

Figure 6.3: Wisdom in the Resistance

With polarities (maybe not with problems, but definitely with a polarity), Johnson is fond of saying there is always wisdom in the resistance. From a leadership perspective, that's quite a switch for some people. Typically, leaders see resistance as anything but wisdom! Instead, they become frustrated that people can't see how clear and logical their solution is. From the leader's diagonal view, everything is incredibly obvious, and those who won't get on board are clearly unreasonable, at best. More often, they see resistors as pains in the neck, breeding negativity and not wanting to make changes for the good of the organization. When they encounter this resistance, they want to push back on it, squash it, and force people to get on board. Thus begins Suffering Paradox.

When viewed through a polarity lens, resistance is seen as reasonable and wise because it can alert the people leading the change to what might happen if they take their solution too far. Think for a moment about what might be different if leaders actually viewed resistance as a sign they need to slow down and look for the wisdom. They could step into a place of curiosity and ask questions that engage the resistance in meaningful dialogue. It's a simple mindset shift that allows us to drive a different conversation about the change.

Driving Different Conversations

One of the most effective ways to lower resistance is to use the method outlined in Figure 6.4 [page 148] and following some form of inquiry like the one outlined in Figure 6.5 [page 149]. This method of using polarities can help get us off our diagonal and asking questions that drive different conversations. We'll look here at several variations of this formula[2] to continue our conversation about change and to examine how to use it in giving feedback and engaging with alternate points of view.

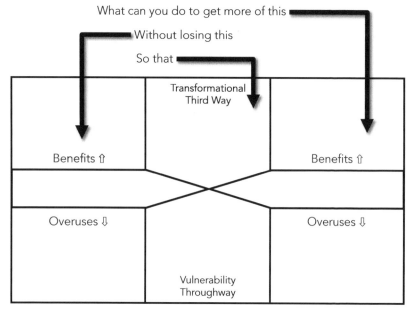

Figure 6.4

Change – Engaging Resistance

During times of change, we can actually intensify resistance when we talk about initiatives on the diagonal. Think about the possible reactions when the founder of a startup asks, "What can we do to move from our inefficient 'everyone has a vote' way of making decisions to a methodical, systematic process with one clear decision maker?" Or when the partner of a law firm announces, "We need to stop operating like a bunch of individuals and start acting as one team." Both of these are clear examples of classic From-To scenarios. We frame a change on the diagonal—we need to stop doing something and start doing more of something else.

The way these questions are asked becomes a setup for treating a polarity like a problem. It's a very common mistake because From-To is completely logical—our either/or mindset takes over and we move quickly to a problem-solving mode that only serves to intensify resistance, slow progress, and create an unsustainable solution. When we use a polarity lens, adopt a both/and mindset, and listen for the wisdom in the resistance, we can ask questions that honor the value and necessity in both perspectives. The key is to be curious and to truly listen. One way to do this is to tee up the question in one of the ways suggested in Figure 6.5: I'm wondering, how can we get *(more of the desired benefits)* without losing *(the benefits of the pole we are currently focused on)*, so that we can *(step into the Third Way)*?

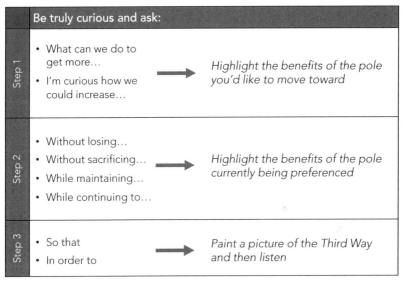

Figure 6.5

For example, what if the founder of the startup instead asked, "How can we get more efficiency in our decision-making process without losing our ability to get the best thinking from the team so that we have streamlined input?" Or if the partner in the law firm asked, "How can we think more like one team without losing our strong sense of individual drive so that we're like a pod of orcas instead of solitary sharks?" What type of change efforts would these questions lead to and how different would they be from the originals above?

Approaches like these are effective because they allow people to focus on "loosening up, not letting go." When we view a polarity like a problem, the solutions we put in place are typically set up in a way that (at least look like) they require us to let go of the pole we are preferencing in order to make the change. We think we have to let go of Empowerment in order to get Control or let go of Individual Focus to be Team Focused. It's no surprise this brings resistance and anxiety to change efforts. With a polarity lens, we can reframe change efforts so that instead of "letting go," our goal becomes getting more of the opposite pole without losing the benefits of the current pole. We loosen up, not lose.

Feedback for Individual Change

The formula above can also hold true for giving constructive feedback. Feedback conversations often involve polarities and, more often than not, the feedback is given on a diagonal. We tell people to stop doing the overuses of a pole and start doing the benefits of the other pole. A manager might say to one of their direct reports, "Your personal brand is suffering. You need to stop driving so hard that you miss the team's social functions (over-focus on Task) and start getting to know your peers across the organization (benefits of Focus on Relationship)." In this case, one of two things could happen. First, the person could swing the pendulum and spend all of their time getting to know their peers, leaving little time to focus on the task at hand. Clearly this is not what the manager is looking for. Getting stuff done and delivering results are important.

More likely, what will happen is the person disregards the valid feedback and continues doing what they've done all along. When getting feedback on the diagonal, people often hear they must sacrifice their values or lose something important to them.

In this case, the direct report might hear, "I have to give up my values of efficiency and productivity in order to build more relationships." The fear of having to sacrifice getting stuff done (the benefits of Focus on Task) or the possibility of getting nothing done (over-focus on Relationship) could cause them to ignore the feedback and drive them further into the overuse of their preferred pole.

A different option would be to deliver the feedback using a formula similar to the one discussed above. In this example, the question might sound like, "What could you do to engage with the team and get to know your peers across the organization *without losing* focus on completing your day-to-day tasks so that you achieve things that people buy into *and* support?" By delivering the feedback using this simple, yet powerful question, we can reduce resistance, increase the probability the feedback will be heard, and expand a person's potential for greater performance.

Alternative Points of View

One of the goals of our work and this book is to provide a tool to help people drive different conversations in their work, lives, and the world—to help them be people who can see and navigate conversations beyond their diagonals. In order to drive these types of conversations, it's first important to acknowledge that our perspective, or the way we see the world, is often on a diagonal. When that diagonal perspective has us instead of us having it, and we bump up against someone holding the opposite diagonal, we are likely to Suffer Paradox unless we can find a way to hold a both/and mindset. To help do that, we can use a version of the formula discussed above to drive a different conversation.

Take the example of Anish who, along with the majority of his team, has a preference for change and Sondra, who has a preference for stability. Anish and the team really like thinking about new and creative ways to do things and don't have a ton of tolerance for the status quo. Sondra, on the other hand, really values predictability, wants to honor the organization's commitment to quality delivery, and doesn't have much tolerance for things that would risk customer satisfaction. One day, as Sondra heads into a team meeting, the entire group is talking about the opportunities being missed by not implementing innovative customer ideas. Anish taps into their energy and starts brainstorming creative ideas to improve the customer experience. During a natural pause in the conversation, Sondra speaks up and reminds the team that "our attempts at implementing new ideas last year ended in a lot of chaos with no real value-add, and we shouldn't risk our current stellar customer quality scores." Anish cuts Sondra short, saying, "You don't get it. Our offerings are becoming stagnant and we need fresh energy—something new and exciting" and then continues the brainstorm. Sondra shifts in her chair, scribbles some notes, and then shares her perspective again, speaking a little louder and a bit slower. "Too many new ideas leaves our employees confused and creates inefficiencies. Our top priority is to ensure quality delivery—you're going to ruin our reputation." Anish doesn't acknowledge the input and continues once again with the brainstorm. Sondra looks down and disengages from the conversation.

This is a classic example of two parties seeing and speaking from their diagonals in a way that leads to Suffering Paradox. It doesn't have to be this way. By making a slight addition to the formula discussed above, we can drive conversations that tap the wisdom of alternative viewpoints (See Figure 6.6).

Suppose Anish engaged in the conversation from a both/ and rather than an either/or mindset—an approach that could potentially expand the perspective of everyone involved. What would be possible if Anish entered the conversation like this: So, what's important to you, Sondra, is making sure that we don't jeopardize our quality delivery and that we maintain our customer-satisfaction scores — that makes a lot of sense. With that in mind, is there a way for us to tap the new energy created by implementing customer ideas without sacrificing our reputation and reliability so that we can be steady *and* progressive?

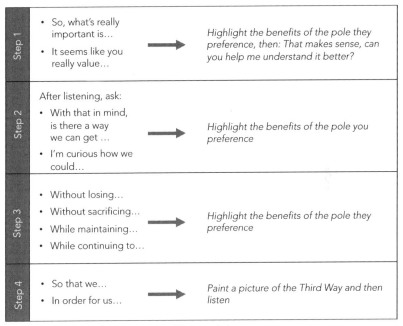

Figure 6.6

Conversely, suppose Sondra had been the one to initiate the conversation by stepping off her diagonal and asking: It seems like you really value new energy and providing creative solutions to our customers. I get why that's important — can you tell me more? (Sondra listens to understand). So, that said, I'm curious how we could ensure we continue our efficient quality delivery while continuing to think of, and implement, new creative ideas in order for us to be reaching and reliable?

Teeing up the conversation in this way does not necessarily mean a solution will be easier to find (though it might be). What it typically does mean, however, is that the people involved will have a different type of conversation. There will be less suffering, with more dialogue, which in turn improves morale, increases communication, and saves relationships. When these things happen, there is a much higher likelihood you'll get better and more sustainable results and be ready to tackle new issues around the corner.

Whether it's laying out alternative conversations, giving feedback, or communicating about change initiatives, knowing how to get curious and step off our diagonal is key to reducing the amount of Suffering Paradox in the world. When we do this, we can spend less time and energy arguing about who's right and more time dealing with the real challenges we're facing. Regardless of your diagonal, it's hard to argue with that.

Conclusion

The goal of this book was to provide an introduction to polarities and how to use the Polarity Navigator as a sensemaking tool to navigate them effectively. It serves as the first in a series of books that explores the multitude of ways polarities play out in different systems and sectors. Our hope is that this first book provides everything you need in order to pick up any of those books and delve more deeply into the topics and areas relevant to your life and work.

Most importantly, our hope is that you are able to use what you've taken from this book and put it into use in your own life. That you are able to navigate polarities more easefully and effectively, and that you can help others do the same. Our goal is to help people understand polarities so they can drive conversations in the world that help alleviate the suffering of polarities and all that it entails. The concepts in this book provide ways to navigate interdependent tensions to greater solutions, stronger relationships, better morale, and richer communication all in the name of sustainable progress. That's what the world is in desperate need of right now.

As the complexity of the world and our problems increase, it becomes easier to be polarized in our views and easier to dig into an either/or mentality. As a result, we *all* suffer. Everyone. Our request is that you use any insights gained from this book to drive different conversations that supplement either/or thinking with both/and thinking in order to help your part of the world navigate and harness the creative tension available to us all.

It can seem overwhelming at times, but we know how to do this. Our discussion began with the Inhale and Exhale dynamic as a way to explore polarities, so we'll end there. Breathing is one of the most effective and practical tools we can use when dialoguing with others, experiencing discomfort, or helping others work through the inherent vulnerability of Navigating Paradox. The breath is with us wherever we go, constantly ready to remind us and always available to us. It is evidence that our bodies know how to find, and stand in, the Third Way if we can trust the unknown and simply inhale...AND...exhale.

LISTS OF POLARITIES

Some Polarities in Organizations

Structure::Flexibility

Employee Interests::Organizational Interests

Continuity::Change

Decentralization::Centralization

Focus on Margin::Focus on Mission

Short-term Focus::Long-term Focus

Participative Leadership::Directive Leadership

Focus on Costs::Focus on Quality

Big Picture::Details

Focus on My Part::Focus on the Whole

Compete with Others::Collaborate with Others

Respect for the Person::Respect for Performance

Reward the Individual::Reward the Team

Integration::Differentiation

Internal Focus::External Focus

Being Relaxed::Being Driven

Do it Differently::Do it Right

Success of Organization::Care for Employees

Focus on Results::Focus on Process

Some Polarities in Leadership

Exude Confidence::Exude Humility

Action::Reflection

Challenge::Support

Focus on Task::Focus on Relationship

Candor::Diplomacy

Implementation::Planning

Grounded::Visionary

Develop Bonds::Maintain Distance

Structure::Flexibility

Stability::Change

Exude Competence::Exude Warmth

Direct Others::Empower Others

Expressive::Contained

Responsibility::Freedom

Individual Focus::Team Focus

Conditional Respect::Unconditional Respect

Go Fast::Go Slow

Realistic::Optimistic

Some Polarities in Life

Work::Rest

Hold Lightly::Take Seriously

Appreciate What Is::Desire More

Focus on Self::Focus on Other

Responsibility::Forgiveness

Reality::Hope

Being Open::Being Assured

Save::Spend

Family::Community
Develop Bonds::Maintain Distance
Individual::Collective
Masculine::Feminine
Learning::Knowing

Some Polarities in Other Systems

Form::Function
Depth::Breadth
Patient Focus::Business Focus
Have the Answers::Let it Emerge
Practice Law::Run a Firm
Go into Details::Keep it Simple
Local Focus::Global Focus
Hold onto Traditions::Embrace the New
Build it::Buy it
Customize::Standardize
Diversified Pipeline::Specialized Pipeline
Focus on Quantity of Life::Focus on Quality of Life
Take Care of My Home::Take Care of the Community
Teach the Students::Learn from the Students
Parent with Unconditional Love::Conditional Love
Focus on the Context::Focus on the Content
Optimize the Trade::Optimize the Portfolio
Develop Technical Skills::Develop People Skills

APPENDIX B

BLANK NAVIGATOR AND TOOL

POLARITY NAVIGATOR

Strategies

Identify actions to stand in the Third Way or step into the Vulnerability

Benefits ⇧

Identify the benefits of healthy-use in this situation

Overuses ⇩

Identify the consequences of overuse in this situation

Transformational Third Way

Identify what it would look like to integrate both poles

Benefits ⇧

Identify the benefits of healthy-use in this situation

Overuses ⇩

Identify the consequences of overuse in this situation

Identify what feels risky about standing in the Third Way
Vulnerability Throughway

POLARITY NAVIGATOR

Transformational Third Way

Pole X

Benefits ⇧
- What benefits occur as a result of focusing on/showing up with this pole?
- What positive impacts does this pole bring to the situation?
- How does this pole contribute to overall success?

Overuses ⇩
- When this pole is overused – when there is too much of it – what happens?
- What occurs when this pole is taken too far?
- What happens when this pole is focused on to the neglect/exclusion of the other pole?

(Third Way center)
- What would it look like/feel like to have the benefits of both poles in this situation?
- What is possible by, or the impact of, harmonizing both poles?
- How do you see the world if you blended X and Y?
- What mindset would result from holding both poles simultaneously?
- What would you be experiencing if you were holding both poles?
- How would other people be experiencing you if you were holding both?

Pole Y

Benefits ⇧
- What benefits occur as a result of focusing on/showing up with this pole?
- What positive impacts does this pole bring to the situation?
- How does this pole contribute to overall success?

Overuses ⇩
- When this pole is overused – when there is too much of it – what happens?
- What occurs when this pole is taken too far?
- What happens when this pole is focused on to the neglect/exclusion of the other pole?

Vulnerability Throughway
- What feels risky about holding both poles together?
- What would you need to "loosen up on" in order to blend both poles?
- What needs to be held, or remembered, to integrate the poles?
- What would be the most uncomfortable part of standing in the Third Way?
- What do you have to be OK with in order to blend both poles?
- What part of who you are, or what you value, needs to shift/expand?
- What's at stake for you if you step into the Third Way?

Strategies
- What actions will you take to achieve the things outlined in the Third Way?
- How could you get more of the benefits of Y without losing the benefits of X?
- What can you do to stay with the vulnerability that arises when pursuing the Third Way?
- How can the tension creatively occupy your heart?
- Movement requires Courage and Comfort. What courageous action is needed to stand in the Third Way – what would Courage do?
- What can you do to experience and act from a place of integration?
- What will you do to Monitor this polarity over time?

NOTES

Introduction

1. Jim Collins, *Good to Great: Why Some Companies Make the Leap – and Others Don't* (New York: HarperBusiness, 2001); Mark Sokol, "Developing polarity thinking in global leaders: An illustration," *Industrial and Organizational Psychology* 5, no. 2 (2012); Wendy Smith and Marianne W. Lewis, "Toward a theory of paradox: A dynamic equilibrium model of organizing," *Academy of Management Review* 36, no. 2 (2011).

2. Andrew Van de Ven and Marshall Poole, "Paradoxical requirements for a theory of change," in *Paradox and transformation: Toward a theory of change in organization and management*, eds. Robert Quinn and Kim Cameron (Cambridge, MA: Ballinger, 1988); Wendy Smith, Marianne Lewis, and Michael Tushman, "Both/And Leadership," *Harvard Business Review*, May 2016.

3. Barry Johnson, *Polarity Management: Identifying and Managing Unsolvable Problems* (Amherst, MA: HRD Press, 1996). The Polarity Map® is a registered trademark of Barry Johnson & Polarity Partnerships, LLC. Commercial use encouraged with permission. www.polaritypartnerships.com

Chapter 1

1. Smith and Lewis, "Toward a theory of paradox."

2. "Hofstede's 6-D Model of National Culture," https://geerthofstede.com/culture-geert-hofstede-gert-jan-hofstede/6d-model-of-national-culture.

3. Jennifer Garvey Berger, *Changing on the Job: Developing Leaders for a Complex World* (Stanford, CA: Stanford University Press, 2013).

4. Beena Sharma and Susanne Cook-Greuter, "Polarities and ego development: Polarity thinking in ego development theory and developmental coaching," https://www.cook-greuter.com/Sharma%20Cook-Greuter%20paper%20EAIF%20SUNY.pdf

5. Johnson, *Polarity Management*.

6. Robert Kegan, *In Over Our Heads: The Mental Demands of Modern Life* (Cambridge, MA: Harvard University Press, 1994).

7. Smith and Lewis, "Toward a theory of paradox."

8. Brian Emerson, "Navigating Organizational Paradox with Polarity Mapping" (PhD diss., Fielding University, 2013).

Chapter 2

1. Johnson, *Polarity Management*.
www.polaritypartnerships.com

2. Richard Rohr, "The Third Way," *Center for Action and Contemplation*, accessed August 26, 2016, https://cac.org/the-third-way-2016-08-26.

3. Doug Silsbee, *Presence-Based Leadership: Complexity Practices for Clarity, Resilience, and Results That Matter* (Ashville, NC: Yes! Global, 2018).

4. Johnson, *Polarity Management*.

5. Hofstede, "6-D Model of National Culture."

6. Robert Kegan and Lisa Laskow Lahey, *Immunity to Change: How to Overcome It and Unlock the Potential in*

Yourself and Your Organization (Cambridge, MA: Harvard Business School Press, 2009).

7. Brené Brown, "Strong Back, Soft Front, Wild Heart," interview by Krista Tippett, *On Being*, Radio Public, February 8, 2018, https://radiopublic.com/OnBeing/ep/s1!ef45f

8. Parker Palmer, *The Promise of Paradox: A Celebration of Contradictions in the Christian Life* (San Francisco: Jossey-Bass, 2008).

9. Brené Brown, *Braving the Wilderness: The Quest for True Belonging and the Courage to Stand Alone* (New York: Random House, 2017).

10. Jennifer Garvey Berger, *Unlocking Leadership Mindtraps: How to Thrive in Complexity* (Stanford, CA: Stanford University, 2019).

Chapter 3

1. Ileana Stigliani and Davide Ravasi, "Organizing Thoughts and Connecting Brains: Material Practices and the Transition From Individual to Group-Level Prospective Sensemaking," *Academy of Management Journal* 55, no. 5 (September 2012): 1232-1259.

2. Smith and Lewis, "Toward a Theory of Paradox."

3. Anne Huff and Mark Jenkins, "Introduction," in *Mapping Strategic Knowledge*, eds. Anne Huff and Mark Jenkins (London: Sage Publications, 2002), 17-32.

4. Garvey Berger, *Unlocking Leadership Mindtraps.*

5. Rohr, "The Third Way."

6. Palmer, *The Promise of Paradox.*

7. Adyashanti, *The End of Your World: Uncensored Straight Talk on the Nature of Enlightenment* (Boulder, CO: Sounds True, 2010).

8. Kim Scott, "Radical Candor," filmed 2016 at INBOUND Bold Talks, video, https://www.youtube.com/watch?v=yj9GLeNCgm4

9. Kegan and Lahey, *Immunity to Change.*

Chapter 4

1. Johnson, *Polarity Management.*

Chapter 5

1. Johnson, *Polarity Management.*

Chapter 6

1. Frank Ostaseski, *The Five Invitations: Discovering What Death Can Teach Us About Living Fully* (New York: Flat Iron Books, 2017).

2. Thanks to the Polarity Mastery community for conversations about Johnson's *Getting Unstuck Process* that sparked the need for these ideas.

THANK YOU AND RESOURCES

Thank you for letting us share our thoughts with you. We hope you choose to join us in the mission of driving different conversations in the world by supplementing either/or with both/and. To assist you in that journey, blank copies of the Polarity Navigator and the Polarity Navigator Tool can be downloaded at www.navigatingpolarities.com. Please sign up for our mailing list and be sure to connect with us on LinkedIn.

Please reach out if you ever have any questions about how you can bring both/and to your part of the world.

—Brian and Kelly

ADDITIONAL BOOKS IN SERIES

This is the first book in a growing series. Each follow-up book, written by other experts in the field, will be short and practical explorations of specific areas or specific polarities. Be on the lookout for these upcoming books:

Navigating Polarities and Global::Local
Navigating Polarities and Coaching
Navigating Polarities In Communities of Faith
Navigating Polarities and Centralization::Decentralization
Navigating Polarities and Adult Development
Navigating Polarities and Leadership

Have a specific topic you'd like to learn more about? Let us know! We're happy to talk about it and will even try to find someone to write a book about it! Reach out at www.navigatingpolarities.com.

ABOUT THE AUTHORS

Kelly Lewis, PCC, is Principal of Lewis Leadership Group, a leadership development and coaching firm committed to helping organizations and individuals uncover their power and joy. Kelly leverages her in-depth knowledge of Polarities and Paradox coupled with her fifteen years as a Fortune 500 executive to help her clients navigate the complexity, ambiguity, and rapid change inherent in organizational life by expanding perspectives and increasing capacity for courageous action. Kelly is honored to serve on Georgetown's Institute for Transformational Leadership faculty and as the Co-Director of the Certificate in Navigating Polarities program. She is a contributing author to *On Becoming a Leadership Coach* (2008). Kelly lives in Richmond, Virginia, with the love of her life and their two furry children.

Brian Emerson, Ph.D. is Principal of Riverstone Endeavors, a firm committed to helping leaders navigate organizational complexity. He has partnered with organizations to achieve sustained results in leadership development, aligning organizational culture and strategy, and harnessing the power of polarities. Brian has studied and worked with polarities for over twenty years and his research yielded the theories of Suffering Paradox and Navigating Paradox. He teaches about paradox in leadership and organizations at the University of Notre Dame, and as co-director of the Certificate in Navigating Polarities at Georgetown University. Brian is the co-author of *A Manager's Guide to Coaching: Simple and Effective Ways to Get the Best From Your Employees*. He lives outside Washington, D.C., where he and his partner are restoring a historic farm and trying their best to keep bees.

.

Printed in Great Britain
by Amazon

65966067R00106